English for Academic Study

New edition

Extended Writing & Research Skills

Teacher's Book

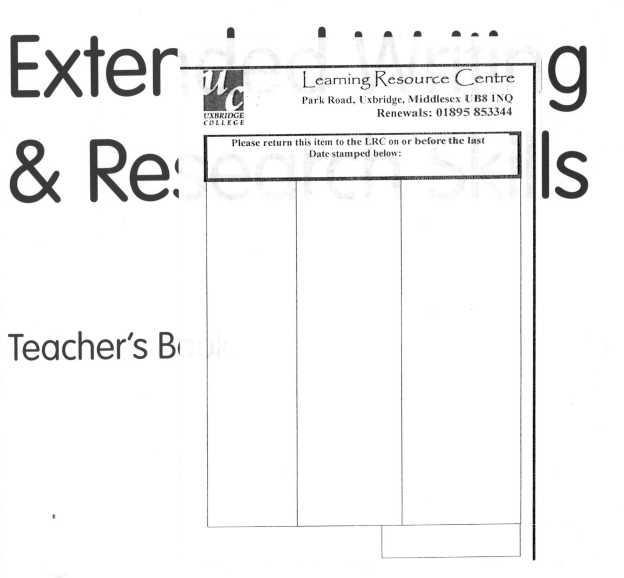
Joan McCormack and John Slaght

ISLC
International Study
and Language Centre

University of
Reading

Garnet
EDUCATION

Credits

Published by
Garnet Publishing Ltd.
8 Southern Court
South Street
Reading RG1 4QS, UK

This edition first published 2012

ISBN: 978 1 90861 431 5

British Library Cataloguing-in-Publication Data
A catalogue record for this book is available from the British Library.

Production

Project manager:	Sarah MacBurnie
Project consultant:	Fiona McGarry
Editorial team:	Kayleigh Buller, Kate Kemp, Clare Roberts
Art director:	Mike Hinks
Design and layout:	Simon Ellway, Ian Lansley, Maddy Lane

Every effort has been made to trace copyright holders and we apologize in advance for any unintentional omissions. We will be happy to insert the appropriate acknowledgements in any subsequent editions.

Printed and bound in Lebanon by International Press: interpress@int-press.com

Contents

Book map

Topic	Tasks
1 Introduction to extended writing and research	■ Critical thinking ■ Thinking about what students in higher education write ■ Types of writing ■ Extended writing ■ Writing a project ■ Analyzing the task ■ Starting a project ■ Unit summary
2 Using evidence to support your ideas	■ Selective reading for source material ■ Incorporating evidence into academic work ■ Referencing ■ Purposeful reading ■ Reading and note-making ■ Stages of writing a summary or paraphrase ■ Practice summary 1 ■ Practice summary 2 ■ Practice summary 3 ■ Unit summary
3 Sourcing information for your project	■ Structuring projects ■ Identifying evaluative writing ■ Developing a stance: Writing a thesis statement ■ Descriptive and evaluative writing ■ Reading for a purpose ■ Reading and thinking critically ■ Choosing sources ■ Finding information ■ Analyzing websites ■ Acknowledging your sources ■ Following academic conventions in referencing ■ Deciding when to avoid using online sources ■ Writing a bibliography ■ Unit summary
4 Developing your project	■ Preparing for tutorials ■ Quotations, paraphrases and plagiarism ■ Avoiding plagiarism ■ Working with abstracts ■ Unit summary

Introduction

Principles and approach

Aims of the course

The purpose of this course is to equip students with the skills necessary for conducting research and for producing a piece of extended writing (referred to here as a project) in their own subject-specific area. The course involves an integrated approach, with a particular focus on the writing and research skills necessary for such a task. The course is designed to encourage critical thinking and get students to be evaluative in their approach to writing. There is also a strong oral component to the course, through discussion of the students' work in class and in tutorials, and at the end of the course, when students practise preparing for a conference presentation.

It is assumed that discrete reading and writing skills, as well as presentation skills, are taught in other components of an English for Academic Purposes (EAP) course. For example, although students will be asked to consider the structure of introductions and conclusions, it will be assumed that they are already familiar with this to some degree. Similarly, although students receive language feedback on their work, they are not explicitly taught grammar in these materials.

Student needs

The following areas have been taken into consideration in the design of the materials, based on an analysis of what students will need to do on future courses:

- the ability to produce an extended piece of writing in their own subject area, within the academic conventions of higher education in English-speaking universities
- the development of discursive skills – to communicate effectively both orally and in writing
- the development of critical thinking skills
- the development of learner autonomy
- an understanding of the conventions of the academic community students will typically be joining
- the development and consolidation of study competencies

Principles on which the materials are based

The learning process as a cycle

Mayes & Fowler (1999) examine how different learning activities enhance students' understanding of new concepts and resolve misunderstandings. They refer to three stages, which are known collectively as the *conceptualization cycle*.

At the *conceptualization stage*, students are exposed to the ideas or concepts of others through lectures, reading and seminar discussion. During the *construction stage*, students apply these new concepts in the performance of meaningful tasks. It is during the *dialogue stage*, however, that learning takes place through the performance of tasks, when these new concepts are tested during written communication and/or conversation with tutors and peers. The feedback provided enables students' misconceptions to be resolved. The approach adopted by these materials is based on similar principles.

Also, the integration of skills from other components of a typical EAP course is an essential aspect of the project preparation class. Students bring with them awareness of the microskills of writing and an awareness of how to use appropriate reading strategies to deal with texts. These are aspects which are recycled in the project class. In this context, writing is learnt rather than taught, because learning how to write occurs through the understanding and manipulation of content.

Reading for the purpose of writing: Writing from multiple texts

The approach taken in these materials is that students are reading to learn, rather than learning to read. To encourage this, students are given a reading purpose: to complete a project (an extended writing assignment). This purpose should generate a 'selective' reading approach, which will help students to deal with the literally hundreds of pages they may be confronted with each week during their future academic courses. It is also generally accepted that teaching students to write from sources is essential preparation for academic success. In his book on the relationship between reading and writing, Grabe (2003) points out the complexity of the process, which involves deciding: how much and which material should be used; how it can be used in relation to the task; how accurately it should be represented; and, finally, the formal mechanisms that need to be used (p. 225).

The process and problem-solving components of writing development can make intense demands on students, particularly when they are reading difficult L2 texts in order to collect or glean new information for their writing. In many reading–writing tasks, students are forced to make a number of complex decisions (Grabe, 2003, p. 245).

It is with this in mind that students are given a range of sources to consider when working on Project 1. The rationale behind this approach is that the teacher has an element of control and can identify ineffective strategies that students may be tempted to employ as a way of coping with multiple, fairly dense academic texts, such as varying degrees of plagiarism.

With Project 2, students will be working with texts in their own subject area and with a much greater degree of autonomy. By this stage, it is hoped that they will have begun to develop the ability to make the 'complex decisions' that Grabe identifies.

A process and product approach

A process approach to writing is advocated, based on research which shows that the process of doing helps the development of organization as well as meaning. It is expected that writing skills will be taught elsewhere, but further development occurs through the process of students completing their project, through drafting and redrafting their work. At each stage of writing, students are encouraged and expected to generate ideas, organize them, evaluate what they are writing and identify clearly what their writing purpose is. Revision is essential, not just to edit the language, but also to reorganize or modify the text and clarify ideas, as necessary, through expansion or rephrasing. At every stage of the process, students are encouraged to critically assess what they have written and to develop this criticality through discussion with their academic colleagues, whether fellow students or teachers.

These materials also strongly emphasize the importance of the end product. This is in line with the needs of students on their future academic courses, when they will have to produce an end product containing some or all of the aspects of academic writing and academic study skills advocated in these materials. Please refer to Appendix 8b (pages 98–99) for an example of how the written project may be evaluated, taking into account not only the content, the use of source materials, the organization and the language of the final draft, but also the actual written presentation of the text and the degree of learner independence exercised by students in producing the final product.

Students finding their own voice

In the complexity of the reading and writing process, students often find it challenging to formulate their own ideas. A strong element of these materials involves getting students to clarify their ideas by voicing them before writing them down. It is important to emphasize to students that even though they are writing in their own subject area, they should be writing with the educated reader in mind, i.e., they should be able to explain their topic to others.

One of the reasons that students plagiarize is that they want to use information they have read to support a point without having fully understood the text. Verbalizing their ideas before writing helps combat this to some extent by helping them clarify their understanding before beginning to write. Students are provided with the texts for Project 1, and are asked to be critical from the beginning. They may be resistant to this approach if they come from a culture where they are not expected to question authoritative sources.

Learner autonomy

Students are expected to be independent learners in higher education. They need to work not only on their study skills techniques, e.g., note-taking and compiling a bibliography, but also on acquiring study competencies which involve the development of critical questioning. Control over one's learning is the basis of learner autonomy; not only attempting to do it, but also actually managing it successfully. However, student attitudes to working autonomously vary in terms of their cultural background, as well as according to the personality of the individual.

The stage of learner autonomy of any student will always be at a certain point along a continuum. The current materials therefore contain 'scaffolded' tasks which provide support throughout much of the course, but which are gradually withdrawn to encourage autonomy, especially during the writing of Project 2. In their article on issues in the EAP curriculum, Flowerdew and Peacock emphasize the importance of this. By asking learners to research and investigate resources available to them inside and outside the academy, as well as encouraging learners to take responsibility for their own learning, teachers will set their students on the path to full independence (Flowerdew & Peacock, 2001, p. 82).

Using *EAS: Extended Writing & Research Skills*

Unit summaries

These provide an opportunity for the students to reflect on what they have done at the end of each unit. You may wish students to complete the unit summaries in class or in their own time. If they complete them out of class, make sure you find time to discuss what the students have done.

The appendices

There are eight units in total, plus the appendices. Each unit focuses on one aspect of extended writing.

Appendix	Content	When to use
1	Sample Project	Unit 3, Task 1, Ex 1.1 and 1.2. However, some teachers may prefer to introduce the project during the first class so that students get an impression of what the final product should be.
2	Self-evaluation checklist	This is probably best introduced in Unit 2, possibly before or after Task 4, as a homework task. As suggested in the instructions on page 127 of the Course Book, students should be encouraged to visit this self-evaluation checklist at appropriate stages throughout their course in order to reflect on their progress. Discussing the checklist could form part of their tutorial time.
3	Taking notes	Unit 2 specifically, but students should be encouraged to refer to this appendix at each stage of their note-taking for Projects 1 and 2, e.g., in Unit 4, with reference to avoiding plagiarism.
4 (4.1–4.3)	Source texts	These should be introduced in Unit 2, when students begin work on Project 1; also during Unit 3, Task 4, in relation to critical reading.
5	Symbols and abbreviations	These should be used when taking notes from texts or lectures; in many cases, there will be subject-specific symbols and abbreviations.

| 6 | Compiling a bibliography | Units 2 and 3, which deal with acknowledging sources and academic conventions in referencing. Unit 4 covers the tutorial system and avoiding plagiarism, and teachers may find it more appropriate to introduce the compilation of a bibliography at this point, or even later in the materials. |

Other features

Glossary: This contains a useful list of terms that the students will need to know during the course.

Study tips: These contain additional information that can be used by the students as a ready reference to a range of study issues related to extended writing and research skills.

Issues

There are certain issues relating to these materials and how they are introduced and used on an EAP course. One issue which needs to be considered is the academic experience and cultural background of the students involved. Secondly, their level of intellectual maturity has to be considered. Both of these issues will impact on the amount of scaffolding which should be given and possibly the extent to which Project 1 should form part of the overall assessment.

Completing Projects 1 and 2

If students follow the whole course, then they are expected to write both Project 1 and Project 2.

Project 1 (about 1,200 words) is carefully scaffolded, and the sources that the students use for their topic are included in the appendices. Units 1–4 of the book introduce a range of extended writing and research skills which can be practised during the completion of this first project; in other words, students are working on Project 1 in parallel with working on the earlier units. It is up to the teacher to decide when to get them started – it could be within the first week. The completion of Project 1 means that students are putting into practice the skills they are developing through working on the earlier units.

For Project 1
- The emphasis is not on teaching writing, but on students putting into practice and consolidating the writing skills they have already been taught.
- Texts are supplied, but students are still expected to use two resources of their own, providing a challenge for stronger students.
- Students are asked to select from a limited number of texts.
- The structure and mechanics are introduced while the project is being written.
- The writing also involves synthesis: bringing together ideas from a range of sources.

The aim then is for students to work on Project 2 (2,000–3,000 words) in their own academic subject area, and for them to develop their independent learning skills while using and consolidating the skills already introduced during the completion of Project 1. Unit 5 should be used to introduce Project 2, and teachers can decide to return to certain tasks covered or passed over earlier if necessary for revision and further consolidation. Teachers might decide to include Unit 6 as part of Project 1, or to wait until the introduction of the second project. Although students will be expected to be more autonomous by this stage, whole class tasks could be attempted from Units 7 and 8, as appropriate. Teachers need to decide whether their students will complete Project 1 before moving on to Project 2, in the individual student's academic area. This will depend on factors such as the length of the course, the number of hours per week dedicated to extended writing and research skills, the level and needs of the students and their previous tertiary-level experience.

For Project 2

- Students look for and use their own resources in their own subject area.
- Students negotiate their own title and specific aim through dialogue with their personal tutor.
- Scaffolding is withdrawn, and students work more independently.
- Class time is mainly concentrated on individual tutorials.
- Students are encouraged to take responsibility for what happens in the tutorial, and guidance on this is given in Unit 4 (Course Book, pages 53–66).

Completing Project 2 only

If students do not need to do Project 1, or if there is insufficient time, teachers are advised to make decisions about a route through the materials, depending on the particular circumstances of their programme. For example, if there is only sufficient time to complete Project 2, then consideration should be given to following the route suggested on pages 12–14 of this book, which proposes that Unit 5 is introduced very early on. This particular route is based on allocation of 30 hours over a 6-week period. It includes preparation for a conference/oral presentation about an aspect of the students' projects, which may be inappropriate for some EAP courses. In such cases, time allocated for this in the suggested route could be channelled into another aspect of the material.

Feedback and assessment

Assessment includes both continuous assessment and assessment of the written project(s), as well as the presentation (Appendices 8a and 8b on pages 97–99 provide the evaluation criteria for these).

Each of the units contains a number of tasks, many of which students could complete outside of class time, to be checked in class. Parallel to this, students are working on their projects, and receive feedback on each stage of the process, e.g., on their initial plan, or on whether the introduction contains a clear focus. Although they may be familiar with the process of peer evaluation in the writing component of their course, the extent to which it is a part of the process of the project class varies according to the individual group. Ideally, it should happen, but if a group is struggling with both the content and the structure of the project, it may be too demanding to expect students to also be involved in effective peer feedback. However, a great deal can be gained from using colleagues as 'sounding boards' to try out ideas and to explain the content as clearly and effectively as possible.

Students should receive both formative and summative feedback on their written drafts of the project from the teacher, and have the opportunity to discuss their work in an individual tutorial. Certain aspects of feedback sessions are particularly significant, for example, written comments on the final project as well as the drafts. Students also need feedback on their oral performance in preparation for their conference presentation. On longer courses, it is often possible to organize 'mock' tutorials as part of the students' spoken language assessment. To make this a more authentic experience, the students' projects can be used as the focus for discussion. Students can be asked to introduce their project, outline the key details and then discuss issues relating to their project with the assessor.

Referencing

The system of referencing used in the materials is that of the APA (American Psychological Association). See a brief summary in Appendix 6 of the Course Book.

A number of the sources included have used different systems; these have been reproduced in the original form. It is worth pointing this out to students, and ensuring they follow the APA system consistently in their own writing of projects.

However, individual institutions or groups may well have their own system. It is important to be systematic and meticulous in the choice and use of the system decided on. Obviously, it is not possible to move between different systems.

Note: In *EAS: Extended Writing & Research Skills*, single quotation marks are generally used to indicate quoted text because this is the publisher's house style. However, the APA referencing system, which is explained in Unit 3, requires double quotation marks.

You may like to explain to your students that, throughout the world, many different referencing systems are in use. The APA and the Harvard (Author-Date) systems are frequently used. It is important for students to check with their departments as to what referencing system is required.

Plagiarism

This is described as a 'sticky issue – not seen as black and white by academics' (Sutherland Smith & Carr, 2005). For example, there is the need to 'imitate in the early stages of learning a new discourse' (Angelil-Carter, 2000). On the other hand, as expressed by Sherman (1992), 'they (the students) find it hard to believe that I really want what I say I want: their own half-formed ideas expressed in their own limited English' (p. 194).

Some students feel that they are representing the writer more fairly by using his/her words. However, the materials aim to raise awareness and develop the skills/techniques to help overcome plagiarism. There is a strong emphasis on being evaluative and on students 'commenting' on what they have read. There is also an attempt to help students develop the skills to be able to express ideas effectively.

Bibliography

Angelil-Carter, S. (2000). *Stolen language? Plagiarism in writing*. New York: Longman.

Flowerdew, J., & Peacock, M. (Eds.) (2001a). *Research perspectives on English for Academic Purposes*. Cambridge: Cambridge University Press.

Flowerdew, J., & Peacock, M. (Eds.) (2001b). The EAP curriculum: Issues, methods and challenges. In J. Flowerdew & M. Peacock (Eds.). *Research perspectives on English for Academic Purposes*. Cambridge: Cambridge University Press.

Grabe, N. (2003). Reading and writing relations: Second language perspectives on research and practice. In B. Kroll (Ed.), *Exploring the dynamics of second language writing*. Cambridge: Cambridge University Press.

Kroll, B. (Ed.) (2003). *Exploring the dynamics of second language writing*. Cambridge: Cambridge University Press.

Lynch, T. (2001). Promoting EAP learner autonomy in a second language university context. In J. Flowerdew & M. Peacock (Eds.), *Research perspectives on English for Academic Purposes*. Cambridge: Cambridge University Press.

Mayes, J. T., & Fowler, C. F. H. (1999). Learning technology and usability: A framework for understanding courseware. *Interacting with Computers, 11*, 185–497.

Robinson, P., Strong, G., Whittle, J., & Nobe, S. (2001). The development of EAP oral discussion ability. In J. Flowerdew & M. Peacock (Eds.), *Research perspectives on English for Academic Purposes*. Cambridge: Cambridge University Press.

Sherman, J. (1992). Your own thoughts in your own words. *ELT Journal 46*(2), 190–198.

Sutherland Smith, W., & Carr, R. (2005). Turnitin.com: Teachers' perspectives of anti-plagiarism software in raising issues of educational integrity. *Journal of University Teaching & Learning Practice, 2*(3), article 10.

Water, A., & Waters, M. (2003). Designing tasks for the development of study competencies. In B. Kroll, (Ed.), *Exploring the dynamics of second language writing*. Cambridge: Cambridge University Press.

Route through the materials

This book is intended to cover, for example, a ten-week course (one whole academic term) of approximately four to five contact hours per week, plus homework. It is assumed that the core microskills of writing are dealt with in another component of the course, e.g., writing introductions and conclusions. This book does not aim to teach these microskills, but rather to reinforce them.

On a full-time course, students could be using the *Reading* and *Writing* books from the EAS series during the morning sessions, for example, and working on the *Extended Writing & Research Skills* materials in the afternoons. The rationale behind this is that students then develop their skills during the *Reading* and *Writing* sessions and put them into practice during the *Extended Writing & Research Skills* sessions.

For ten-week courses, for example, one unit per week should be covered, based on three 90-minute periods per week. However, it may only take nine weeks to cover the actual material, and students will spend the rest of their time working on their own projects. The final week will be mainly individual tutorials, with little class input, as students will be working independently.

It is assumed that students completing a course of eight weeks or more will complete all units of the book and tasks to suit their needs. On pages 12–14 is a suggested route for students undertaking a course of six weeks or fewer. It is based on the assumption that they will have six hours of tuition per week.

The Course Book provides links to other EAP materials at www.englishforacademicstudy.com. Students should be encouraged to work on these materials, either for homework or as self-study support work.

Note: On a short course, it is important to explain the purpose of the project preparation class in the first lesson. Explain that the tasks are designed to help the students develop the skills they need. It is also important to explain that the materials have been designed for much longer courses, so some of the contents may be omitted; point out, for example, that they will only be writing Project 2 (in their subject area). Finally, explain that some of the work may not follow the order of the book.

Date	Lesson content	Homework
Week 1		
Session 1	■ Explain aims and objectives of the project class ■ CB Unit 1, Task 5 (pages 15–16): *Writing a project* ■ **Note:** Remember to give out written language assignment for students to complete for negotiated deadline.	■ CB Appendix 2 (pages 127–128): Self-evaluation checklist ■ Read through Unit 1 for consolidation ■ Students search for sources in their subject area
Session 2	■ Briefly refer to self-evaluation checklist in CB Appendix 2 (pages 127–128) ■ CB Unit 5, Introduction and Task 1 (pages 67–68): *Choosing a topic for your extended essay* ■ CB Unit 5, Task 3 (page 69): *Establishing a focus* ■ CB Unit 5, Task 4 (page 70): *Establishing a working title*	

Session 3	■ CB Unit 2, Tasks 2 and 3 (pages 23–26): *Incorporating evidence into academic work; Referencing*	■ Complete unfinished work from Unit 2, Tasks 2 and 3 ■ Research for project ongoing
Week 2		
Session 1	■ CB Unit 3, Task 1 (page 35). *Structuring projects* ■ CB Unit 3, Task 2 (page 36) *Identifying evaluative writing*	■ CB Unit 3, Task 8 (pages 43–46): *Finding information.* Students should read carefully for negotiated deadline and complete the task
Session 2	■ CB Unit 3, Tasks 10 and 11 (pages 48–50): *Acknowledging your sources; Following academic conventions in referencing*	■ Planning and making notes for first draft
Session 3	■ CB Unit 4, Tasks 2 and 3 (pages 56–58): *Quotations, paraphrases and plagiarism; Avoiding plagiarism*	■ Writing first draft ■ Writing first draft (to be submitted by negotiated deadline
Session 4	■ Unit 6, Introduction and Task 1 (pages 74–79): *Features of introductions*	
Week 3		
Session 1	■ Tutorials	■ Students respond to tutorial comments
Session 2	■ Tutorials	■ Students respond to tutorial comments
Session 3	■ CB Unit 6, Tasks 5–7 (pages 82–87): *Features of conclusions; Analyzing your conclusion; The language of conclusions*	■ CB Unit 7 (pages 93–102) Students should read contents of the unit
Week 4		
Session 1	■ CB Unit 8, Introduction (pages 103–104) ■ CB Unit 8, Task 1 (pages 104–105): *Identifying the features of abstracts*	■ CB Unit 8, Task 2, Ex 2.1 (pages 106–108): *Conference abstracts*
Session 2	■ Return first drafts and make general comments ■ Distribute written feedback sheets ■ CB Unit 8, Task 2, Ex 2.2 and 2.3 (page 108): *Conference abstracts*	■ Writing second drafts; must respond to comments on feedback sheets
Session 3	■ Submitting abstract	■ Conference presentation abstract deadline

Session 4	■ Tutorials: discuss second drafts; students bring feedback sheets	■ Writing second drafts
Week 5		
Session 1	CB Unit 8, Task 6 (pages 113–114): *Editing your written work*	■ Writing second drafts
Session 2	■ Catch-up ■ Second draft peer evaluation; concentrate on introductions and conclusions ■ Discuss presentations; familiarize students with assessment forms	■ Complete second drafts for negotiated deadline
Session 3	■ Tutorials and catch-up	■ Presentation preparation
Session 4	■ CB Unit 8, Task 3 (pages 109–110): *Preparing an oral presentation*	■ Presentation preparation
Week 6		
Session 1	■ Course evaluation questionnaire ■ Feed back to individuals about project, as appropriate	
Session 2	■ Conference presentations: Students base their presentations on an aspect of their projects	

Introduction to extended writing and research

1

In this unit students will:

- become more aware of what extended writing involves
- find out about a writing project

Introduction

This unit introduces students to extended writing and informs them about the projects they will work on in this book. The term *project* is used throughout the course because the main focus of the course is to complete either one or two projects/pieces of extended writing.

Introduce the course by explaining that it will help students to develop practical skills for extended writing. They will also learn to carry out research in the library and online, so that they have the necessary information to tackle extended essays. Refer students to the Contents and Book map pages of the Course Book (pages 3–5) for the area of focus of each unit, and to the Introduction (pages 7–8) for the aims of the Course Book and the skills it will help them to develop.

`INPUT` Academic disciplines on the typical university campus

You could ask the students to briefly introduce themselves and explain which academic discipline they are studying or intend to study within. If they are postgraduate or doctoral students, they might want to say a little bit about their research interests.

`INPUT` Extended writing at university: Why do students write?

Briefly talk through the reasons why students carry out extended academic writing listed on Course Book page 10 and explain that these translate into different types of writing for different purposes. Highlight that the students will have the opportunity to practise each of these types of writing during this course.

Task 1 | Critical thinking

1.1   You could ask the students if they can think of another example of when they use critical thinking skills in their daily life. They might find it easier to understand the concept if they first consider it this way before moving on to the more abstract uses of critical thinking in academic contexts. For example, if we need to buy some food but we only have a small amount of money, we would need to think critically about what food is the best value and most likely to be satisfying.

Possible answers:
- recognizing relevant information
- identifying the writer's purpose
- assessing the writer's argument critically
- comparing and evaluating issues
- evaluating the credibility of a writer's sources
- detecting bias
- differentiating between main and supporting ideas
- justifying ideas, comments and analyses used by a writer

Task 2 | Thinking about what students in higher education write

2.1 Ask students to write for no more than five minutes. Quickly ask around the class for suggestions about the type of writing they might have to do at university.

Possible answers:
- extended essays or projects
- theses
- dissertations
- reports
- case studies
- notes
- annotations (e.g., on handouts, photocopied originals, etc.)

Write up the students' ideas on the board, but don't add any at this stage as they will get more ideas in Ex 2.2.

2.2 Get students to read the boxed text on page 11 in order to compare their ideas with what is written there. Elicit any other types of writing that are mentioned in the Course Book and add them to the list on the board.

2.3 The types of writing that students will do depends to some extent on the academic department that they will join. Students should identify which types of writing listed on the board they are likely to engage in.

> **Language note:** *Thesis* vs *dissertation*
>
> The terms *thesis* and *dissertation* are used differently in different countries and even in different universities in the same country. In most universities in the UK, Hong Kong and Australia, a thesis is written for the research degrees of PhD and MPhil, while a much shorter dissertation is one of the final requirements for a taught Master's degree. In many American universities the terms are reversed, with theses written at Master's level and a doctoral dissertation at PhD level. For our purposes, the Hong Kong, UK and Australian terms for a PhD thesis and a taught Master's dissertation are used. See Bunton, D. (2002). Generic moves in PhD Introduction chapters. In J. Flowerdew (Ed.), *Academic discourse*. London: Pearson Education.

Task 3 | Types of writing

3.1 This task is meant simply to enhance students' understanding of the types and length of writing they may have to do. It also clarifies the level of study at which the various types of writing are practised. The sample answers on the next page are repeated as a photocopiable handout in Appendix 1a on page 23.

Possible answers:

Type of writing	Level of student (undergraduate/ postgraduate/doctoral)	Explanation
essay for examination	undergraduate/ postgraduate	traditional 600–1,000-word text written during an exam
lab report	undergraduate/ postgraduate/doctoral	written-up accounts of work done under experimental conditions – of particular relevance to students in the scientific disciplines
field study report	undergraduate/ postgraduate/doctoral	combines theoretical analysis with observation and practice, e.g., a report written about work experience carried out as part of a university Business Studies course
PowerPoint slide	undergraduate/ postgraduate/doctoral	normally contains brief, bulleted notes used to support the information and ideas being explained by a teacher/lecturer during a class, or by presenter in a seminar at a conference
wiki	undergraduate/ postgraduate/doctoral	a wiki is a collaborative website which can be directly edited by anyone with access to it
blog	undergraduate/ postgraduate/doctoral	a kind of online journal or diary which anyone can read; it may include a comments facility so that readers can comment on specific posts
extended essay/ project	undergraduate/ postgraduate	written work submitted as part of the course requirement during term-time – typically a piece of work 600–6,000 words long
thesis	doctoral	doctorate level: this will be much longer than a dissertation
dissertation	undergraduate/ postgraduate	Bachelor's level: usually 10,000–12,000 words Master's level: 15,000–20,000 words
report	undergraduate/ postgraduate	describes research; a piece of informative writing that describes a set of actions and analyses any results in response to a specific brief
case study	undergraduate/ postgraduate	an account that gives detailed information about a person, group or thing and its development over a period of time
notes	undergraduate/ postgraduate	information recorded from written sources, lectures, seminars or tutorials, for later reference
annotations	undergraduate/ postgraduate	comments, explanations or highlighting added to written sources or lecture handouts

It would be worth going through the notes here on the process that all of these types of writing will have in common: gathering ideas, organizing them into a plan, drafting and redrafting.

You could also highlight that a key part of extended writing and research is being able to communicate the research that you do to other people, both through written essays, articles and papers and orally through presentations and discussions.

INPUT Types of assessment

Explain to students that they can find out what type of assessment is used in their individual departments by checking the appropriate handbook. The Meteorology Department at the University of Reading, for example, provides an online handbook that contains information on assessment. An alternative may be to check in the relevant undergraduate or postgraduate prospectus. However, information on assessment is not consistent and is not always present.

The best way to find out about the expectations of written assessment is for the student to visit his or her particular university department and ask for samples of assessed written work. Emphasize that all three forms of assessment mentioned on page 13 of the Course Book are equally important.

You may need to explain that continuous assessment is based on how students carry out their research, organize their time and work, and how they cooperate with fellow students and teachers, as well as on attendance and participation in class activities. Emphasize the link between written and spoken language components of any course. Explain that students are expected to put the lessons of other components of their course into practice when working on projects or written tasks.

Extension activity: A course conference

You may choose to hold a conference at the end of the course, where all students are expected to give an oral presentation (of about 10 minutes) or a poster presentation. Advice on how to prepare for a poster presentation is given in Unit 8 of the Course Book. If you are planning to do this, it might be a good idea to inform your students of this right at the beginning of the course, so they can have this in the back of their minds as they progress.

Task 4	Extended writing

It would be worth spending some time here talking through the way that the course will work and emphasizing to students that they will need to do a considerable amount of independent study outside of class.

4.1 Highlight that they will be using the *process approach* to writing or *process writing approach*. Ask the students to consider what this involves. They may find it easiest to draw a diagram to illustrate this. Please refer to Appendix 1b on page 24 for an example diagram.

You could elicit ideas and build these up into a diagram on the board, showing how the different tasks involved move on from one another, but also linking them with arrows to show that they will have to return to earlier parts of the process – possibly several times – before they will have a finished text.

There is no need to go into too much detail about what each part of the process entails at this stage. They will focus on this in Task 5.

4.2   Point out that while this and future academic courses will involve a high degree of independent study, their tutors will be there to support them. They should try to think of at least three things they might want to discuss.

Possible answers:

- how to write an appropriate introduction and conclusion
- thesis statement
- logical organization of ideas
- appropriate use of academic conventions and style
- introduction and conclusion
- appropriate use of sources

[INPUT] Projects 1 and 2

Go through the information on pages 14–15 of the Course Book with the students and answer any questions they may have. Explain that they will be able to practise one-to-one tutorials in Unit 4, but will also be having such tutorials with you at regular intervals during the course.

Note: While working on projects, students should make good use of tutorial sessions by preparing any questions in advance.

For students using this book for a longer 8-week or 11-week course, the written project should be regarded as practice for a second assignment. Students on a shorter 5-week course will only have time to complete one compulsory project.

Task 5	Writing a project

The aim of this task is for students to discuss and cooperate in the decision-making process. Explain/review that there are three distinct stages involved in the writing process: planning, researching and writing up. Within each stage, there are also a number of phases or steps. Make sure students appreciate that certain phases can occur in more than one stage.

Before you set this task, check/explain the key terms below:

- rough outline
- establishing a clear focus
- working title
- sources
- tutorial

5.1   Remind students to write out the steps in full; *not* to simply write down the number of the steps, as this provides a better reference for future use.

> **Methodology note: An alternative procedure***
>
> Photocopy and cut up the sentences in Appendix 1c on page 25. Put the students in groups of three to four students and give them the jumbled slips of paper. They write the headings *Planning, Researching* and *Writing up* on this piece of paper and stick the slips on with glue according to where they belong. Students can then make a poster with arrows, linking lines, etc., to help visualize the writing process. Make it clear that students will probably have different views.
>
> *Thanks to Jonathan Smith at ISLC for this idea

5.2 Arrange the class in pairs or groups to discuss the possible stages in the answer key. Ask students if there are any stages that they think are missing from the phases. Finally, ask how the third *writing up* phase would continue, i.e., *write second draft*; *read draft*; *edit*, etc. (The process should be repeated as necessary.)

The answer key below is open to discussion and this should be made clear to the students.

Possible answers:

Planning

1. 10) Decide on a topic.
2. 16) Check that sources are available/accessible.
3. 3) Think of a working title for the project.
4. 15) Make a rough outline plan of your ideas.
5. 14) Work on establishing a clear focus.
6. 13) Plan the content in detail.

Researching

1. 4) Search for relevant journals/books/information in the library and on the Internet.
2. 5) Write down the details of your sources.
3. 9) Do some reading.
4. 12) Highlight/take notes of relevant information.
5. 6) Decide if you need to do more reading.

Writing up

1. 11) Write the first complete draft.
2. 1) Read the first draft.
3. 2) Edit the draft – decide objectively whether your ideas have been expressed clearly.
4. 8) Arrange a tutorial with your tutor.
5. 7) Write the contents page, bibliography, title page and abstract.

Task 6	Analyzing the task

6.1 As this is the first time the students have done this kind of title analysis on this course, it would be a good idea to spend some time identifying the key words and establishing exactly what the title is asking them. This will be followed up with a focus on deconstructing project questions in Task 7.

Answers:

1. The title is framed as a statement, followed by a question:

   To what extent …?

   Make sure that students fully understand the statement and encourage them to provide examples of current policies *in any discipline* that might impact on future generations.

2. Remind students that a question requires an answer. Elicit a range of answers that the question *To what extent …* might produce, e.g., *a great deal, quite a lot, not much, not at all*. Explain to students that they must decide *To what extent* through their research and then they must explain their answer in their project, using the evidence in the sources they are given to support their argument.

Task 7   Starting a project

Deconstructing the project question

Students often start writing about a topic before really considering what they are required to do. This task takes students through the process of deconstructing project questions and analyzing exactly what is being asked of them.

7.1   Encourage the students to work individually before comparing answers in pairs or small groups. They should try to think of as many questions as they can. They will select from these in the next exercise.

Possible answers:

4–6

- If energy is the key factor, what can be done to meet this need?
- Is 'recycling' an effective policy?
- How damaging is deforestation?
- What is 'food security'?
- How important is 'food security'?

7.2   Emphasize to the students that, at this stage, they should be thinking as widely around the topic as they can. They will be narrowing their focus as they continue planning and doing their reading and research. The more ideas they have at this stage and the more ways they can think of to approach the question, the easier they will find it to identify information in the reading texts which might be appropriate for the project.

At this stage, they should be aiming for a very loose plan – it's worth pointing out that they will revisit this many times, adding in and deleting ideas as they go along. It's important that the students become comfortable with the idea and importance of revision and editing at this early point in the course.

Extension activity

If you wish to give students further practice in deconstructing project questions, below are three essay titles you might like to use.

You could ask the students to do this task in groups. Depending on the amount of time you have, you could ask each group to look at just one of the questions and deconstruct it, before reporting back to the whole class.

Possible answers:

Food science

Childhood obesity is on the rise worldwide. Discuss some of the reasons for this.

- What is a definition of 'obesity'?
- What is a definition of 'childhood obesity'?
- What evidence is there of a rise in obesity?
- Why is it on the rise?
- Is the cause lack of exercise / fast food / the impact of the digital age / ignorance about the causes of obesity?

Finance and investment

Analyze the causes of the credit crunch/crash of 2007–2008. What has been its most significant consequence?

- What were the causes?
- Which was the main cause?
- What were/have been the results of the credit crunch?
- Were the short-term or long-term consequences?
- Which result had the most dramatic impact?

Applied linguistics

What makes someone a good language learner? Is this something a teacher can influence?

- What is the definition of a 'good language learner'?
- What are the main reasons why some people are good language learners?
- Is gender a factor? If 'yes', what evidence is there to support this?
- Is living in the target language country a major factor?
- Is it the teacher or the teaching method which makes a good language learner?

Unit summary

You may want the students to complete the unit summaries in class or in their own time. If they complete them outside of the class, make sure you get some feedback during class time.

You may wish to set up some of the tasks, either to clarify what to do, or to help get students thinking about the topics.

Some of the items can be done individually and others are best done in pairs or groups. When working outside the classroom, encourage students to find the time to meet with others and complete any pair or group activities.

1 **Answers:**
- a. develop
- b. provide
- c. dispute
- d. display

2–3 **Answers:**
Answers depend on students.

4 **Possible answers:**
- a. decide on a topic / check that sources are available / think of a working title for the project / work on establishing a clear focus / plan the contents in detail
- b. search for relevant information / write down details of sources / highlight or take notes of relevant information / do some reading / decide if you need to do more reading
- c. write the first complete draft / read the first draft / edit the first draft / arrange a tutorial with your tutor / write the contents page, bibliography, title page and abstract

5 **Answers:**
Answers depend on students.

Appendix 1a

Type of writing	Level of student (undergraduate/ postgraduate/doctoral)	Explanation
essay for examination	undergraduate/ postgraduate	traditional 600–1,000-word text written during an exam
lab report	undergraduate/ postgraduate/doctoral	written-up accounts of work done under experimental conditions – of particular relevance to students in the scientific disciplines
field study report	undergraduate/ postgraduate/doctoral	combines theoretical analysis with observation and practice, e.g., a report written about work experience carried out as part of a university Business Studies course
PowerPoint slide	undergraduate/ postgraduate/doctoral	normally contains brief, bulleted notes used to support the information and ideas being explained by a teacher/lecturer during a class, or by presenter in a seminar at a conference
wiki	undergraduate/ postgraduate/doctoral	a wiki is a collaborative website which can be directly edited by anyone with access to it
blog	undergraduate/ postgraduate/doctoral	a kind of online journal or diary which anyone can read; may include a comments facility so that readers can comment on specific posts
extended essay/project	undergraduate/ postgraduate	written work submitted as part of the course requirement during term-time – typically a piece of work 600–6,000 words long
thesis	doctoral	doctorate level: this will be much longer than a dissertation
dissertation	undergraduate/ postgraduate	Bachelor's level: usually 10,000–12,000 words Master's level: 15,000–20,000 words
report	undergraduate/ postgraduate	describes research; a piece of informative writing that describes a set of actions and analyses any results in response to a specific brief
case study	undergraduate/ postgraduate	an account that gives detailed information about a person, group or thing and its development over a period of time
notes	undergraduate/ postgraduate	information recorded from written sources, lectures, seminars or tutorials, for later reference
annotations	undergraduate/ postgraduate	comments, explanations or highlighting added to written sources or lecture handouts

PHOTOCOPIABLE

Process Writing Approach

Process writing on an extended writing and research programme involves several stages. At every stage, revisions to the content, organization and language of your project will be required. You will be expected to review and rewrite at every stage of the process, depending on the feedback you receive from your teacher and the information and ideas that evolve from your research and during the reading and writing process. Study the diagram below:

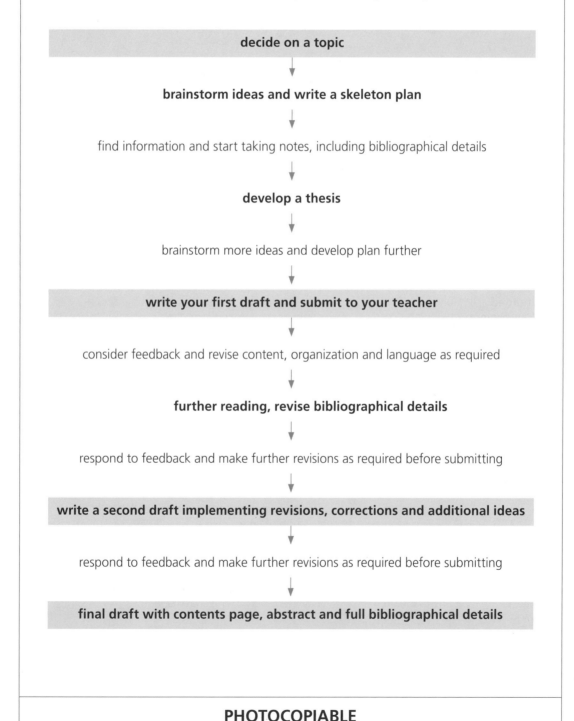

decide on a topic

↓

brainstorm ideas and write a skeleton plan

↓

find information and start taking notes, including bibliographical details

↓

develop a thesis

↓

brainstorm more ideas and develop plan further

↓

write your first draft and submit to your teacher

↓

consider feedback and revise content, organization and language as required

↓

further reading, revise bibliographical details

↓

respond to feedback and make further revisions as required before submitting

↓

write a second draft implementing revisions, corrections and additional ideas

↓

respond to feedback and make further revisions as required before submitting

↓

final draft with contents page, abstract and full bibliographical details

PHOTOCOPIABLE

Appendix 1c

1. Read the first draft.

2. Edit the draft – decide objectively whether your ideas have been expressed clearly.

3. Think of a working title for the project.

4. Search for relevant journals/books/information in the library and on the Internet.

5. Write down the details of your sources.

6. Decide if you need to do more reading.

7. Write the contents page, bibliography, title page and abstract.

8. Arrange a tutorial with your tutor.

9. Do some reading.

10. Decide on a topic.

11. Write the first complete draft.

12. Highlight/take notes of the relevant information.

13. Plan the content in detail.

14. Work on establishing a clear focus.

15. Make a rough outline plan of your ideas.

16. Check that sources are available/accessible.

PHOTOCOPIABLE

INPUT Incorporating evidence

You can use these examples to work through the different ways of incorporating evidence, as detailed in the text following this exercise in the Course Book.

> **Methodology notes: Focusing students' reading of the Input texts**
>
> You could write some short questions on the board for students to answer as they are reading the Input texts to help focus them. For example, for the text on *Incorporating evidence,* you could ask to them to tell you:
>
> 1. What are the three ways of incorporating evidence?
> 2. What is the difference between a *global* summary and a *selective* summary?
> 3. What is the difference between *paraphrasing* and *summarizing*?
> 4. Which method should you use the *least* frequently? Why?
> 5. What do you need to remember to do in each case?
>
> **Answers:**
>
> 1. The three ways of incorporating evidence are summarizing, paraphrasing and using direct quotations.
> 2. A global summary summarizes a whole text, while a selective summary summarizes part of a text.
> 3. Paraphrasing usually refers to writing about a writer's specific idea in your own words, whereas summarizing usually refers to writing about the general messages or tone of what a writer has written.
> 4. It is better not to use direct quotations too frequently. It's much better to put things into your own words, and too many direct quotations can make your text difficult to follow.
> 5. You need to remember to acknowledge the source of the idea in all three ways of incorporating evidence.

Task 3   Referencing

Students may have been introduced to identifying information in texts and summarizing ideas in *English for Academic Study: Writing.* Emphasize that writing a project gives them the opportunity to put into practice the skills they are being taught in other components of their course. Evidence of appropriate referencing is expected in their projects, and is essential in academic writing.

Although many people find referencing straightforward, you may find that some students struggle with both the concept and format of references in academic writing, particularly if they come from a culture where it is not considered necessary or important to acknowledge other people's work. It's important to take time to go through these exercises carefully.

Note: All referencing examples in this series follow the American Psychological Association (APA) referencing style. However, there are other referencing styles, which are discussed in Unit 3, Ex 13.3.

3.1   References to be highlighted are given in the first column of the table below.

3.2   Make sure that students understand the difference between a *direct* reference and an *indirect* reference.

3.3   This will focus students' attention on the key ideas expressed by each of the sources referenced in the extract.

Answers:

Name and date (Ex 3.1)	Direct/indirect reference (Ex 3.2)	Idea expressed (Ex 3.3)
O'Riordan, 1976	indirect	5
John Muir (quoted in Pepper, 1984)	direct (this is an example of the writer quoting a source that has been quoted in a previous work)	4
Ronald Inglehart, 1977	indirect/direct (short phrases quoted directly but general point paraphrased)	3
Maslow, 1970	indirect/direct (as above)	1
Cotgrove & Duff, 1980	indirect/direct (as above)	6
Downs, 1972	indirect	2

Task 4   Purposeful reading

4.1   You could get students to transfer two of the definitions they find in the source texts to a table, such as the one below. A blank version of this is available to photocopy (Appendix 2a, page 36). You may wish to direct students in particular to the sources on Wikipedia, UK Gov and in Appendix 4.2 (*Sustainability: science or fiction?* by Pim Martens).

Definition	Author	Date	Title	Page number	Source of publication
Sustainable development is 'simply this: to provide for the fundamental needs of humankind without doing violence to the natural system of life on earth.'	Martens, P.	2006	Sustainability: science or fiction?	pp. 36–41	*Sustainability: Science, Practice, & Policy*

5.1 Please note that students should complete Ex 5.1 before looking at the Input panel.

The students can do this task individually before comparing ideas in pairs or in a small group. They should use the information in the Input box to help them.

INPUT Summarizing information

Summarizing may have been covered in other components of the students' course; however, it is worth going over the points made here to refresh their memory. It is a good idea to emphasize that students should summarize from their notes, partly in order to help them summarize in their own words. If students try to summarize directly from the text, the outcome is often too close to the original in terms of vocabulary and structure.

It is essential to remind students always to note the source of their summaries. The source still has to be acknowledged, even if students write the summary in their own words – the ideas are the 'intellectual property' of the original writer. It might be an idea to highlight the term *plagiarism* here. This will also be covered in more detail in Unit 4.

Students usually find the task of summarizing information – trying to express a set of ideas in their own words – extremely challenging. At times, it can be difficult to convince them that incorporating information from texts into their own work without referencing is not academically acceptable. The aim of this section is to take the students through some steps to make summarizing easier, and to raise their awareness of the dangers of plagiarism.

Two key factors should be emphasized throughout:

- Students should have a purpose when they summarize, e.g., presenting a writer's viewpoint, which they may support or disagree with.
- Students need to interact with the text in some way in order to fully comprehend it, i.e., think carefully about the meaning. Emphasize that it is not useful to attempt to summarize if they have not fully understood the text. For this reason, it can be very useful to have students verbalize the ideas first, explaining the content of what they have read before they actually write.

5.2 The aim of this task is to raise awareness and generate discussion.

Answers:

1. This is not necessary, unless there is a set of steps or a process that logically needs to have the same order as the original.
2. No. The point of the summary is to choose what is relevant for the reader's purpose.
3. No. It is important to emphasize that specialist vocabulary is essential, and cannot be changed. Clarify that a summary should be in the students' own words, but not to the extent that they use inappropriate vocabulary in order to avoid the words in the text. Point out here that actually telling someone their ideas can be helpful; students will thus avoid using too much of the same vocabulary.
4. Yes. This will probably occur naturally if students are writing from their notes.
5. Yes. Part of the skill of summarizing is emphasizing the important points (but without directly saying *I think this is important*).
6. Any comment or opinion needs to be separate from the summary itself. The student may be required to comment on the content of the summary and/or give their own opinion or viewpoint in a different section of the task or project.

| Task 6 | **Stages of writing a summary or paraphrase** |

Tasks 6 and 7 look at the N O W approach to summarizing and various methods of note-taking, starting with the Cornell note-taking system outlined in Appendix 3 (Course Book, page 129). Mind-mapping and regular linear note-taking are also presented.

Encourage students to consider their preferences in terms of note-taking. They should think about the method they currently use and also which aspects of the methods introduced they might find most useful.

> **Methodology note: The stages of the N O W approach to summarizing**
>
> As an alternative to simply asking the students to read through the notes on the N O W approach to summarizing, you could give them a cut-up matching task to do.
>
> Photocopy and cut up enough sets from Appendix 2b on page 37 so there is one for each group of three to four students. With their books closed, ask them to put the sentences into three groups: (1) Making notes, (2) Organizing the notes and (3) Writing up the notes. They should also put the sentences into the correct order within these groups.
>
> They can then check their answers with the information on page 28 of the Course Book.

Appendix 3: Taking notes

You may like to refer students to Appendix 3 (Course Book, pages 129–130) at this stage, for some advice on taking notes. Suggested answers to the tasks in Appendix 3 appear below.

Task 1: Taking notes when listening or reading

Students discuss the differences between taking notes while listening to a lecture compared with while reading.

Possible answers:

Listening	Reading
You cannot underline key words or annotate what you hear.	You can underline/highlight the text to help you decide what is important for your notes.
You cannot listen ahead to see whether a point is developed more later on.	You can read ahead to see whether ideas are further explored later in the text.
You need to write as quickly as you can.	You can take your time.
You will probably need to copy out your notes again as you will be using symbols and abbreviations to help you write quickly.	You probably only need to make one copy of your notes.
You cannot ask others for help if they have not heard the same lecture/programme/seminar as you.	You can ask others to help you understand parts of the text that you don't understand, at a later date.
You can sometimes ask the speaker questions to clarify what they have said.	You usually cannot ask the author to explain points that they have written.

Task 2: Discussion

Student answers will vary here. You might like to ask them to consider the differences that they have identified in Task 1 to help focus their thinking.

Task 3: Note-taking strategies

Again, student answers will vary. You may prefer to keep this discussion quite open, encouraging students to share ideas but without giving too much input until the students have worked through the rest of the relevant material in Unit 2. Following this, you could ask them to return to this task and expand their notes accordingly.

6.1 The aim of this task and the following ones is to encourage good summarizing practice. The students can work through the steps in this first task in pairs or small groups. It is useful for them to work through the process together, as a model for future reference. Highlight that the notes they are working on are taken from the underlined sections of the text on pages 24–25 of the Course Book.

Note: Refer students to Appendix 5 in the Course Book (pages 149–150) for a set of symbols and abbreviations that they can use when making notes and which will help them to understand notes prepared by someone else.

Possible answer (Step 3):

Note that this text is also reproduced in a photocopiable handout in Appendix 2c on page 38. The natural environment has always been an important issue for <u>two</u> reasons. It provides essential <u>resources</u> required for economic growth and is also a place of beauty where people find "spiritual nourishment". During the <u>1960s and 1970s</u>, concern for the environment grew. Some feel this was a result of society becoming increasingly aware of the <u>damage</u> being done and the need to <u>protect</u> and preserve it for future <u>generations</u>. However, others argue that support for <u>environmental</u> issues has been linked to times of <u>economic</u> growth predominantly within developed countries and among the <u>wealthier</u> and more highly educated in those societies. Debate continues as to whether it is economic prosperity or "social introspection" which affects society's <u>attitudes</u> to the environment.

Task 7	Practice summary 1

7.1/ Emphasize the importance of keeping in mind their purpose for reading as they work with
7.2 the text on page 30 of the Course Book. Not everything in this text will be relevant to the particular aspect of the project question they are focusing on here.

7.3 You will need to go through the principle of mind-mapping with your students if they are not already familiar with the technique. If this is the first time they have done this, they may find it easier to work backwards, using the notes in Ex 7.4 to complete the mind map to see how the ideas can be shown to interrelate and connect with one another.

Answers:

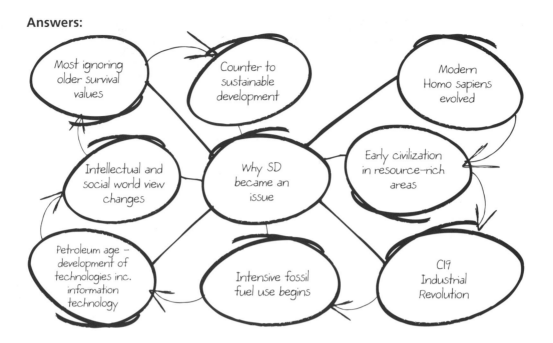

7.4   As mentioned above, students may find it easier to use the notes to complete the mind map if they have not used this method of note-taking before. If they do the mind map first, they should check that there isn't anything important here which they have left out.

7.5   Encourage the students to use the notes they have made in their mind map to complete this text, referring back to the source text only if absolutely necessary.

Answer:

Summary

The evolution of modern man (Homo sapiens) meant increased use of natural resources. However, the intensive use of such resources started when the Industrial Revolution began, and this demand has been dramatically increasing during the Information Age, more accurately referred to as the Petroleum Age. Meanwhile, many of the traditional survival values have been replaced by intellectual and social world values which run contrary to the needs of sustainable development.

Task 8	Practice summary 2

8.1   Encourage the students to use the same techniques they have been using so far to focus their reading on the specific question asked and underline only information that will be relevant to their answer.

8.2   You may like to ask the students to do this task in pairs. They will have an opportunity to apply the skills they have been learning to some individual work in Task 9.

The students can use either a linear note-taking method or experiment with a mind map.

Possible answer:

One of the causes of animal species becoming extinct is termed 'undercrowding' (Barnett, 2001). This is the opposite of overcrowding and is where a species has a low population density within a given area. Although it may seem logical that a smaller population will mean greater access to food and other resources for these survivors, a sharp decline in a population can in fact present a major risk to the species. This is sometimes referred to as one of the 'Allee effects' after the biologist Warder Allee, who first highlighted this paradox more than 50 years ago.

[INPUT] The Cornell Note-Taking System

Point out to students that the [N] [O] [W] approach can be supported by the Cornell note-taking system. Discuss with students why using the left-hand 'annotations' column could be beneficial. Remind students they need to interact with a text in order to understand it, as it is difficult to summarize without full understanding. The process of annotating notes as suggested by the Cornell system encourages this.

Task 9	**Practice summary 3**

9.1   Before students begin Task 9, encourage them to consider their note-taking preferences. First, they should think about the note-taking methods they have used up to now and how successful these have been. Second, they should consider whether the methods they have practised in Unit 2 have helped. You may like to ask students to do this in small groups before discussing as a class.

Students should complete Task 9 individually, putting into practice the skills they have learnt during this unit. You could follow this up by asking the students to read each other's summaries in pairs, as well as giving the students some feedback yourself.

Unit summary

1   Students may choose any of the reasons on page 21 of the Course Book that they marked as being of high importance.

2   Students should draw on the information on page 22 to help them answer this question. Good advice includes:
- considering the purpose for reading before they begin
- paying closer attention to sections of high relevance compared with those that are not useful
- trying to identify which sections are useful from the table of contents/index before they begin reading
- taking notes and summarizing sections as required
- making a note of source information and integrating this into their notes

3 It is important that any claim, opinion or generalization made in an essay is supported by <u>evidence</u>. You need to show <u>proof</u> that what you are saying is correct. To incorporate evidence into your writing, you can <u>paraphrase</u> a specific idea from the writer in your own words or you can <u>summarize</u> the content of a text (write a shorter version that concentrates on the main information). Occasionally, you might want to use direct <u>quotations</u> (the writer's exact words). When you use other people's ideas, you must <u>acknowledge</u> them. This means referring to them both within the text and in a bibliography at the end of the text.

4 Answers depend on students. It would be a good idea to ask them to share their answers either in groups or with the whole class.

Transfer two of the definitions you find in the source texts to the table below. Use the example to help you.

Definition	Author	Date	Title	Page number	Source of publication
Sustainable development is 'simply this: to provide for the fundamental needs of humankind without doing violence to the natural system of life on earth.'	Martens, P.	2006	Sustainability: science or fiction?	pp. 36–41	Sustainability: Science, Practice, & Policy

PHOTOCOPIABLE

Appendix 2b

Making notes

Identify your note-making purpose, e.g., to summarize the whole text (a 'global' summary), or specific parts of the text that are relevant to a particular purpose (a 'selective' summary).

Find the relevant main ideas and underline them.

Write out the underlined section in note form, using your own words where possible.

Check the original text to make sure that you have not missed out any important information relevant to your purpose.

Organizing the notes

Study the notes and decide in which order you wish to put the information when you write the summary. This will depend on why you are making the notes; for example, whether you want to produce a global or selective summary of the original text.

Decide how you want to prioritize the information. You may want to reorganize the ideas and information, or decide that some of it is not relevant.

Organize the notes according to your purpose; you may wish to rewrite them or put them in the form of a mind map.

Writing up the notes

Write up the notes to produce your summary text. Remember that you are transforming the notes from note form into full, connected sentences.

Edit your first draft; make sure you have included all the relevant information and checked the accuracy of your grammar, vocabulary and spelling.

Write out a second draft, if necessary.

PHOTOCOPIABLE

The natural environment has always been an important issue for <u>two</u> reasons. It provides essential <u>resources</u> required for economic growth and is also a place of beauty where people find "spiritual nourishment". During the <u>1960s and 1970s</u>, concern for the environment grew. Some feel this was a result of society becoming increasingly aware of the <u>damage</u> being done and the need to <u>protect</u> and preserve it for future <u>generations</u>. However, others argue that support for <u>environmental</u> issues has been linked to times of <u>economic</u> growth predominantly within developed countries and among the <u>wealthier</u> and more highly educated in those societies. Debate continues as to whether it is economic prosperity or "social introspection" which affects society's <u>attitudes</u> to the environment.

3 Sourcing information for your project

In this unit students will:

- look at how a project is structured
- learn to identify evaluative or critical writing
- practise academic referencing
- practise selecting information from websites

Introduction

The aim of this section is to familiarize students with a typical first project. The length, features and format of the sample project *To what extent should insider dealing be regulated, and how can this be done effectively?* in Appendix 1 (Course Book, pages 120–126) make it a reasonable approximation of what students should be aiming for.

The project was completed by a pre-sessional student and was chosen because it is about a fairly accessible topic, but contains some useful examples of academic style and conventions (e.g., quotations and a bibliography). It is also generally well organized, with an introduction, a main body and a conclusion. This project will be of particular interest to students planning to study economics or finance.

Task 1 Structuring projects

1.1 This is intended purely as a familiarization task, so that students have a clear idea of typical components of the project they are expected to write. Discuss the parts of an academic text, as listed in the Course Book, before students look through the project.

You could ask students to 'storyboard' an academic text, drawing rectangles to represent thumbnails of the pages. These could be labelled with the appropriate parts (e.g., introduction, thesis statement, conclusion, bibliography, etc.). This would provide further scaffolding before the students go on to examine the project in the next exercise.

1.2 Allow students some time to look through the project and label the various parts. Several of the sections, e.g., the introduction, abstract and bibliography, are already appropriately headed, but others, such as quotations, references in the text or subtitles, do have to be identified. It would be a good idea to put the class into groups of three or four students and then circulate and confirm that every student has labelled the various sections of the project appropriately. Students may find it useful to use highlighters to do this.

Emphasize that they may not find all of the items listed in this example.

2.1

> **Methodology note: Working as a whole class**
> For a change of pace, you may like to ask the class to do this task together. Enlarge the list of examples of descriptive and evaluative writing on the photocopiable handout in Appendix 3a on page 48 and cut them into strips. Hand out the sentences to the class. Divide the board into two halves and label them 'Descriptive writing' and 'Evaluative writing'. Ask the students to stick their strips in the appropriate section. When they have all been stuck on the board, ask them to review their work together and check that they agree that all the sentences are in the correct place.

It is worthwhile to point out the importance of students being evaluative or critical in their writing from the beginning. They should establish a clear focus and develop a strong thesis for their project. The writer's 'position' should be a thread that runs through the whole essay, giving it cohesion and coherence. The example of the plan for the project on the restructuring of the South Korean banking system in Ex 3.4 illustrates this very clearly.

Answers:

Descriptive writing	Evaluative writing
1. lists ideas, information or facts **3.** identifies different factors involved **9.** outlines what has been observed **11.** shows the order in which things happen **12.** describes a process or a situation	**2.** explains the reasoning/rationale behind a theory **4.** shows why something is relevant or suitable **5.** evaluates links between different information **6.** places ideas or concepts in their order of importance **7.** explains the significance of information or ideas **8.** compares the importance of different factors **10.** discusses the strengths and weaknesses of ideas or concepts

Task 3   **Developing a stance: Writing a thesis statement**

3.1 Ask the students to consider the example project title and thesis statement in pairs or groups. Discuss ideas of how they lead from one to the other as a class. They should notice that the thesis statement essentially answers the question posed by the project title.

3.2 Ask the students to read the explanation about thesis statements and then explain what they have understood to a partner. You could also ask one or two students to share their summary of the main points with the whole class to give you an indication of how much they have understood the points made here.

3.3   Students can discuss their answers to these questions in pairs or small groups. It may be a good idea to make an OHT (or other visual medium) of the flow chart on page 38 of the Course Book, and display it for general discussion.

Answers:
1. The four boxes entitled: Introduction; Main body, first section; Main body, subsequent sections; and Conclusion refer to the actual written content.
2. It is very important to continue critical reading throughout the development of the text so that the writer can continue to add ideas, check understanding and look for supporting evidence.
3. A description, because it will be important to explain the context briefly before developing the main thesis and arguments.

3.4   Student answers will vary. You may like to discuss this question as a class, encouraging students to share ideas.

| Task 4 | **Descriptive and evaluative writing** |

The purpose of this task is to help students identify the different features of descriptive and evaluative writing, and this should be pointed out. Some paragraphs will be mainly descriptive but have some evaluative elements, while paragraph 4 is predominantly evaluative, and forms the conclusion to the article.

Note that the *Banking system developments in the four Asian tigers* is taken from an American publication and therefore spelling and punctuation follow American English conventions.

4.1/
4.2   **Answers:**

Paragraph	Mainly descriptive (D)	Evaluative comments (E)
1	✔	✔
2		✔
3	✔	✔
4		✔

4.3   Refer students to the photocopiable handout in Appendix 3b on page 49.

Ask the students to identify and underline the evaluative writing in these extracts. Students may also identify the language that shows caution on the part of the writer (which is often typical of academic style), using a highlighter.

Explain that the text they have underlined is evaluative because it generally expresses an opinion or attitude about the facts that are given in the rest of the text.

Answers:
Paragraph 1
Because of the new investment opportunities they provide and because their experiences **may** offer lessons for less developed economies …

Paragraph 2

These numbers <u>make it clear that</u> external trade has been <u>an important element</u> in the development of these economies.

Paragraph 3

Commercial banks <u>also played a critical role, because they were the major source</u> of private savings.

Paragraph 4

The figures **seem** <u>to reflect</u> the emphases of the past development policies. 'The financial system <u>was rather the accommodator of this real economic performance than its instigator,'</u> wrote one economist after examining the role of the financial sector in economic development experiences of these economies (Patrick, 1994). Recent banking sector developments in South Korea and, to a lesser extent, Taiwan, <u>point to the negative side-effects that government direction of credit to preferred industries can have in the long run.</u> Singapore's experience seems to suggest that a government **could** implement industrial development policies without directing the credit decisions of the commercial banking sector. Finally, Hong Kong's case **seems to** <u>illustrate that</u> an active industrial policy **may** **not** <u>be essential</u> for rapid economic development.

Task 5	Reading for a purpose

Reading for a purpose is a key concept and this section reinforces the work students may have previously done in *EAS: Reading* and *EAS: Writing*.

5.1   This task prepares the students for Ex 5.3. Give them one minute to write down some ideas to answer the question and then share them with a partner.

5.2   This text relates to the emphasis on critical thinking which underpins the course, and should be crucial to how students approach both their reading and writing.

Extension activity

Ask students to discuss whether they already find themselves using this approach as they read. Ask them to find the three things the text suggests they do to help them read critically (paragraph 2).

Answers:

1. Decide whether a text is useful or not as you begin reading.
2. Decide whether or not you agree with what is being said.
3. Relate what you are reading to what you already know.

> **Study skills: Labelling themes in students' notes**
>
> It's important to emphasize that students need to make links between the points made in the different source texts that they read for their project. One way to do this is to identify key themes and label these clearly within their notes whenever they come up, perhaps using different colours or highlighters to make them easy to see and refer back to.

| Task 6 | **Reading and thinking critically** |

Ask the students to explain the differences between *critical reading* and *critical thinking* to a partner. Emphasize that they should explain this in their own words.

6.1 You may choose to look at the sentence as a whole class and analyze it together. Ask them which words in the sentence may require further definition (critical reading) and then decide whether they agree or disagree with the statement and why (critical thinking).

| Task 7 | **Choosing sources** |

The purpose of this task is to get students to think about the selection of texts for their work. For this project, all the texts are chosen for them, but for the second project (if students are doing the longer course), and indeed for future projects, they will need to find sources for themselves.

7.1 The students should evaluate if the reasons listed for why this text was chosen are valid by looking at the text and the reference given for it.

7.2 **Possible answers:**

Text 1	Adapted from Martens, P. (2006). Sustainability: science or fiction? *Sustainability: Science, Practice, and Policy, 2*(1), 36–41.
Why it was chosen	■ a Google search shows that the author has published widely ■ it was written relatively recently ■ an academic source, so the information is likely to be reliable and accurate
Text 2	Adapted from Fusco Girard, L. (2006). Innovative Strategies for Urban Heritage Conservation, Sustainable Development, and Renewable Energy. *Global Urban Development, 2*(1), 1–9.
Why it was chosen	■ title of article contains key words related to the project title, e.g., 'conservation', suggesting keeping /maintaining things for the future ■ a Google search shows that the author has published widely ■ article was written relatively recently ■ source is academic, so the information is likely to be reliable and accurate ■ appears to be written for any reader with an interest in the topic, not just the subject specialist

Students will probably already have had a library introduction at some point. Increasingly, students tend to use web-based sources for their work, and avoid using the library. However, their future departments will expect them to be fully familiar with how to use the library facilities, and the location of journals and books related to their subject area.

8.1   Many students will say that they 'think' about the topic, but don't normally write anything down. It may be a good idea to discuss the pros and cons of doing this as a class.

> **Study skills: Keeping an annotated list of references**
>
> It may be useful for students to consider keeping an annotated list of the texts they look at where they can write brief notes on the content and relevance of the book or document. This will help them if they need to go back to the literature at any point to look for further information. Often the title of a paper or book does not tell us how relevant the text will be for the particular purpose we have for reading.

8.2   Check that the students understand the terms written in bold here (e.g., title, blurb, index, etc.)

You may like to ask them to consider which of these parts of the text they regularly check already to help them select a text.

8.3   This can be completed as a homework task or combined with a library induction, as appropriate. Highlight that they should find two books that are relevant to their subject area. Alternatively, they could look for texts that will help them with their first project, as they are expected to find two texts for this themselves, to use alongside the provided core texts.

Filling in the table requires students to think about their selection of sources, which is one aspect of developing critical thinking.

8.4   Encourage students to find out which journals are favoured by their departments. Articles can be useful as the starting point for research, and abstracts are invaluable in ascertaining if an article is relevant to a student's purpose.

INPUT Finding information

At this point, it might be a good idea to show the students an example of an online library page and its search facility, perhaps the one attached to either the university where the students are studying at the moment, or one that they intend to go to.

8.5   Students will need to refer back to the information in this table during Task 9.

9.1   Check that students are familiar with using search engines before asking them to do this task, perhaps for homework. You may need to suggest that they input the search terms within quotation marks to help them narrow their search.

9.2 Students will need to refer back to the information given in Ex 8.5 to help them complete the tables.

Possible answers:

Title	Education for sustainable development
URL	http://www.unesco.org/new/en/education/themes/leading-the-international-agenda/education-for-sustainable-development/three-terms-one-goal/ and http://www.unesco.org/new/en/education/themes/leading-the-international-agenda/education-for-sustainable-development/
Authority	Information is produced by UNESCO, which is generally considered a reliable organization.
Date	The most recently updated source.
Content	Focus on the most relevant issue, suggesting that education is particularly relevant in determining that the needs of the future will be safeguarded, and this suggests the need for a long-term policy.
Accuracy/ reliability	The organization is a recognized, reliable source of information.
Audience	Accessible to the educated reader.
Further comments/ notes	Encourage students to make their own personal comments, e.g., what they think of a particular text and how the ideas here relate to others they know about already.

Title	Sustainability: science or fiction?
URL	http://sspp.proquest.com/archives/vol2iss1/communityessay.martens.html
Authority	Likely to be reliable as it was written by an eminent academic. The article is from an academic journal, which means it should have been peer-reviewed and undergone close scrutiny.
Date	Published in 2006, thus relatively current.
Content	The brief historical overview of sustainable development is followed by an emphasis on the idea that for any plan to be fully effective, it needs to go through two generations, and a whole new approach is introduced with an integrated approach to tackling the problem.
Accuracy/ reliability	From an academic source; will have been carefully reviewed and edited. Twelve detailed references included in the bibliography.
Audience	Accessible to the educated reader; no apparent agenda, especially as some of the author's suggestions would not be popular with some.
Further comments/ notes	Encourage students to make their own personal comments, e.g., what they think of a particular text and how the ideas here relate to others they know about already.

Task 10 — Acknowledging your sources

Tasks 10 and 11 build on the work that was done on referencing in Unit 2.

10.1   Ask the students to work on this individually before discussing their ideas in pairs or small groups. They will then compare their answers to those given in the Course Book in Ex 10.2.

Answers:
Reasons for referencing sources:

- To show where your ideas originated – acknowledging the source.
- To give your writing academic weight.
- To show awareness of other writers' opinions or views.
- To allow the reader to find the original source.
- To avoid plagiarism.

10.2   There is further input on referring to sources using quotations, paragraphing and summarizing in Unit 2.

Task 11 — Following academic conventions in referencing

Note: As mentioned in the Introduction, single quotation marks are generally used to indicate quoted text because this is the publisher's house style. However, the APA referencing system requires double quotation marks.

Again, as mentioned, you may like to explain to your students that throughout the world many different referencing systems are in use. The APA and the Harvard (Author-Date) systems are frequently used. It is important for students to check with their departments as to what referencing system is required.

11.1   Highlight that in all of the examples of using direct quotations, the source is acknowledged by writing the author's family name, the year of publication and, usually, the page number the quote is taken from. Page numbers may not always be possible, for example, if the quote is taken from a website.

Point out that page numbers are not normally given when the writer summarizes or paraphrases what he or she has read, rather than including a direct quotation.

> **Methodology note: Writing quiz questions on the Input texts**
> You may like to ask your students to read the information about direct quotations, paraphrasing and summarizing and write three questions to test the other students on their understanding. The students can then share their questions with the rest of the class, who try to answer them.

Task 12 — Deciding when to avoid using online sources

12.1   Ask the students to share their reasons for why this is important. Highlight the importance of using *credible* sources and the fact that many websites can be written by non-experts, although they may pretend to be, and therefore contain false information, and/or may be considerably out of date.

It may also be a good opportunity here to highlight the pros and cons of using a website like Wikipedia. You may like to ask your students for their opinions on the credibility of the information contained there and explain that many university departments will suggest that students do not use it as a source for academic work.

Task 13	**Writing a bibliography**

Highlight again that there are two parts to referencing: in-text citations (acknowledgements within the body of the text) and the bibliography or reference list that comes at the end of the project or essay.

13.1   **Answers:**
1. title of article   d
2. name of publisher   j
3. date of publication   c
4. author's surname   a
5. title of book   h
6. editor's surname   e
7. place of publication   i
8. author's initials   b
9. other editors   f
10. shows book is a collection of articles   g

13.2   This task acts as a further orientating exercise before the students identify the problems and errors in the bibliography in Ex 13.3. Refer students to Appendix 6 in the Course Book for a brief summary of the APA (American Psychological Association) system of referencing.

13.3   Highlight that students will need to check that the punctuation as well as the content is in the correct order and all the information needed is given.

Note: Page numbers should not be included when referencing an entire book, as shown in the answer for the first entry. Also, the place of publication is missing for both the first and the third entries in the information provided in the Course Book. These have been included in the answers below. In similar circumstances, students would need to find missing information (such as place of publication) for the APA referencing system, and should be aware of the particular requirements of any other referencing system they use.

Answers:

Bilham-Boult, A. et al. (1999). *People, Places and Themes*. Portsmouth: Heinemann.

Harch, E. (2003). *Africa Recovery*. Retrieved May 18, 2004, from www.africarecovery.org

Newman, P. (1999). Transport: Reducing automobile dependence. In D. Satterwaite (Ed.), *The Earthscan Reader in Sustainable Cities* (pp. 67–92). London: Earthscan Publications.

Refer to pages 10–11 of this Teacher's Book and remind students about the use of different referencing formats in different universities and faculties (e.g., the Harvard system, the Chicago system, and the Institute of Electrical and Electronics Engineers (IEEE) system, etc.).

Unit summary

   Answers:

1–4   Answers depend on students. You may want to encourage them to share their answers with you, perhaps by sending you a short e-mail, or sharing an entry in a learning journal.

Identifying evaluative writing

1. lists ideas, information or facts

2. explains the reasoning/rationale behind a theory

3. identifies different factors involved

4. shows why something is relevant or suitable

5. evaluates links between different information

6. places ideas or concepts in their order of importance

7. explains the significance of information or ideas

8. compares the importance of different factors

9. outlines what has been observed

10. discusses the strengths and weaknesses of ideas or concepts

11. shows the order in which things happen

12. describes a process or a situation

Based on ideas from Cottrell, S. (2008). *The study skills handbook.* Basingstoke: Palgrave Macmillan.

PHOTOCOPIABLE

Appendix 3b

Underline the evaluative text and highlight the language that shows caution in these extracts.

Paragraph 1

Because of the new investment opportunities they provide and because their experiences may offer lessons for less developed economies …

Paragraph 2

These numbers make it clear that external trade has been an important element in the development of these economies.

Paragraph 3

Commercial banks also played a critical role, because they were the major source of private savings.

Paragraph 4

The figures seem to reflect the emphases of the past development policies. 'The financial system was rather the accommodator of this real economic performance than its instigator,' wrote one economist after examining the role of the financial sector in economic development experiences of these economies (Patrick, 1994). Recent banking sector developments in South Korea and, to a lesser extent, Taiwan, point to the negative side-effects that government direction of credit to preferred industries can have in the long run. Singapore's experience seems to suggest that a government could implement industrial development policies without directing the credit decisions of the commercial banking sector. Finally, Hong Kong's case seems to illustrate that an active industrial policy may not be essential for rapid economic development.

PHOTOCOPIABLE

4 Developing your project

In this unit students will:

- find out how to make the best use of the tutorial system
- learn about plagiarism and how to avoid it
- learn about the features of abstracts and their purpose

Introduction

INPUT The tutorial system/Making the best use of tutorial time

Some students may be unfamiliar with having one-to-one tutorials. It's important to emphasize the need to be well prepared in order to get the most out of these sessions.

It's also worth mentioning that students will probably not be the tutor's only tutees, and that they will not be able to organize a tutorial whenever they like.

Task 1   Preparing for tutorials

1.1   The main aim of this task is to encourage students to consider what aspects of the feedback they might want to follow up in a tutorial.

You could use either the Essay Feedback Sheet that is given in the Course Book on pages 53–54 or make up an example using the feedback sheet that the students will receive from you or another department in your university.

Ask the students to share their ideas as a class. It may be worth highlighting that in a tutorial, the tutor is not there to 'do the work for them', but to support and guide them. So, for example, following up on the feedback in the Language section of the feedback sheet, it would not be a good idea for the student to turn up at the tutorial and ask the tutor to explain the use of *according to*. A better approach would be to research the use of this phrase beforehand, and then use the tutorial to check that he/she now understands how to use it correctly.

> **Content**
> A major problem with the projects produced by pre-sessional students is that they tend to be over-descriptive. There is very little discussion involved. One way to encourage comments is to get students to answer questions about the topic of their project.
>
> **Example procedure:**
> - Write the title of the project on the board: *To what extent can the problems of urban development be met by a policy of sustainable development?*
> - Underline the phrase *To what extent*.
> - Draw a line on the board and label it with the phrases *not at all* and *completely* at appropriate ends of the continuum.
> - Write the phrases: *quite a lot; to a certain extent; a bit; to a great extent*, in random order.
> - Get students to choose one of these phrases in order to answer the question.
> - When students have made their choice about the 'extent', get them to answer the question *Why?*
> - Tell students to write down the term *because* and below it write between three and five reasons taken from the evidence they have been reading as research.

Example: *Because of the efforts made by international organizations, such as Greenpeace, to encourage sustainable development.*

- As an extension, you could write the word *however* and ask students to write alternatives to the points they have written under *because*. The end result might look something like this:

because:

- *of the efforts made by international organizations, such as Greenpeace, to encourage sustainable development*

however:

- *sustainable development policies are very expensive to introduce, especially in less economically developed countries (LEDCs)*

Organization

A project should be organized in such a way that the main ideas are clear and linked to the introduction and conclusion. The text should be coherent, i.e., there should be a logical development of ideas. The text should also be cohesive, i.e., the ideas in the text should be connected linguistically through the use of appropriate linking words, anaphoric and cataphoric referents, etc.

Language

Students should be issued with error correction codes. This helps them to identify the types of errors they have made and is a step towards independent error correction. Error correction codes tend to work most efficiently with higher-level students and are a useful instrument to encourage independent editing. However, it is important to point students in the right direction for any remedial language work needed. This can be achieved both through the error correction sheet and through written comments on the feedback sheet about certain language issues they might address (see the example on pages 53–54 in the Course Book).

Presentation of work

This has become less of a problem as students now submit their work electronically. However, they need to be given advice about such things as which fonts and font size to use, as well as style, headings and subheadings, bullets and numbering, pagination, the incorporation of tables and figures, and the incorporation of footnotes.

Use of sources

Students must be convinced that the use of sources is an essential requirement of academic writing. Referencing/citing and bibliographies are dealt with in Units 2 and 3, as well as this unit. Students should be encouraged to follow the appropriate academic conventions appropriately and consistently.

| INPUT | Avoiding plagiarism

Highlight the fact that taking good notes will be invaluable at the writing stage. These should clearly show which sections are direct quotations and what the student has paraphrased or summarized from the source texts, with all the bibliographical information recorded for easy reference. This will help students to avoid plagiarism.

| INPUT | What is plagiarism?

It is important to refer to this concept throughout the course. Some students will not have come across this before, particularly the idea that even if you paraphrase or summarize someone else's words, they still need to include an acknowledgement.

It is also worth pointing out that plagiarism does not just mean copying from published texts. It can also refer to copying another student's work and claiming it as one's own. Some universities use sophisticated software to check essays against submissions in previous years and essays available on the Internet. It would be a good idea to highlight this.

The aim of this task is to get students to identify examples of quotes and paraphrases and also to recognize where plagiarism has occurred. Ask the students to read the text carefully and more than once so they will be better able to assess the students' writing in the next exercise.

INPUT Why you must avoid plagiarism

It might be a good idea here to show the students the plagiarism policy of the institution you are working within. They may not be aware of the severity of the consequences that plagiarism could have.

Task 2	Quotations, paraphrases and plagiarism

2.1 Ask the students to decide if the extracts contain a quotation or a paraphrase.

2.2 Once they have identified whether any parts of the extracts are directly copied from the text, they should decide if it counts as an example of plagiarism or not.

Remind students of the need to include direct quotations within quotation marks, as well as including details of the source of the information.

Answers (Ex 2.1–2.2):

	Quotation or paraphrase	Plagiarism	Comment
1	paraphrase	✔	The student has attempted to paraphrase the original text but some words are too close to the original – key phrases have been copied directly, e.g., *i.e., without damaging the environment.*
2	paraphrase	✘	The student has reworded the text so that it is sufficiently different from the original, but has also acknowledged the source of their information.
3	quotation	✘	The words are directly quoted, but this is indicated by the punctuation and the source is acknowledged. Point out to students that quotes of 40 words or more should form a separate paragraph, and should be indented as demonstrated in Unit 3.
4	paraphrase	✔	The ideas of the original are maintained without acknowledgement, although the wording is completely different.
5	paraphrase	✘	Here the student has referred to the source but has not paraphrased the key ideas well. It seems that he/she has not understood the distinction between the two types of building.

Task 3 | Avoiding plagiarism

The aim of this task is to reinforce awareness of plagiarism.

3.1/ 3.2 Each 'reason' for plagiarizing could be discussed, initially by the students in pairs and then as a whole class. They can make notes of the advice they might give on the form on page 58 of the Course Book. There will be a variety of responses. Below are some suggested responses.

Possible answers:

1. Lack of awareness of rules: *I didn't know it was wrong.*
   Advice: Explain the reasons why copying text/paraphrasing too closely is wrong.

2. Lack of familiarity with how to reference: *I don't know how to use references, or how to cite my sources.*
   Advice: Read through material on how to reference appropriately, e.g., in this Course Book.

3. Lack of time: *I don't have enough time to do the necessary reading, or to develop my own ideas.*
   Advice: Work on your time management. Reprioritize the course work – it's essential to do the reading to make the financial input and time worthwhile. Make use of the strategies discussed in earlier units of the Course Book on selective reading.

4. Level of difficulty of reference text: *The text was so difficult for me to understand that I just copied the text and hoped it was OK.*
   Advice: There are no short cuts, so if you don't understand the text, either don't use it, or consult someone who does. Focus on your reading strategies and skills. There are lots of good materials to help you with this. Try to talk through what you have read about with other students to check your understanding.

5. Inability to express ideas better: *The text I copied said exactly what I wanted to say, and I couldn't express it better.*
   Advice: It's OK to include some direct quotations, but these must be appropriately marked. Try taking notes and then work from these when writing up. This might help you to see how you can write in your own words.

6. Different cultural experience: *In my country, we are expected to reproduce the exact words and ideas of the text or the teacher.*
   Advice: In most English-speaking universities, it is more highly valued to be able to give your own ideas and opinions that are based on evidence and facts you have read and are able to acknowledge.

Task 4 | Working with abstracts

INPUT What they are/How they are used
You could ask your students to summarize the Input text in 100 words or less. While it won't be the same as an abstract, it could be a useful exercise in summarizing and encourage students to think about how researchers choose what is relevant when writing a summary of a longer paper.

4.1/
4.2

You may want to ask the students to highlight or underline the different features they might expect to find in an abstract in the input text before they look at the examples of abstracts on page 60 of the Course Book.

Ask the students to label the various features of Abstracts A and B in the margin of their book (in pencil). Encourage discussion about their findings.

For lower-level groups, you could ask the students to look at the list of features on page 61 and identify the ones they find in each of the abstracts.

Answers:

Abstract	A	B
1. a general statement/essential background information	✔	✔
2. the aims of the project, dissertation or thesis	✔	
3. the implementation of an investigation in a real-world situation		
4. how the text is organized		
5. details of research carried out by the writer		✔
6. what the results of the research suggest		✔
7. a thesis statement	✔	✔
8. a definition		

4.3

Abstracts D and E are from academic articles, and students may find the language challenging. However, it is good for them to realize fully what they will be faced with once they embark on their academic courses. These abstracts also demonstrate that while we teach students the 'rules' of academic writing, these are not always followed.

Answers:

Abstract	C	D	E	F
1. a general statement/essential background information	✔	✔	✔	✔
2. the aims of the project, dissertation or thesis			✔	✔
3. the implementation of an investigation in a real-world situation			✔	✔
4. how the text is organized	✔			✔
5. details of research carried out by the writer				
6. what the results of the research suggest				
7. a thesis statement		✔	✔	
8. a definition	✔	✔		✔

Note: In Abstract C, there is no reference to details of specific research carried out by the writer. It suggests that the writer is only reviewing existing literature.

In Abstract D, it suggests that the writer is reviewing existing projects and highlighting the strategy, as opposed to reporting on the results of new research.

4.4   This task encourages students to look for the overall message of the abstracts and to further summarize the content into a single 'headline'.

Possible answers:

Abstract	Possible title
A	Computer-based Testing versus Traditional Testing
B	Assessment Criteria for Observed Teaching Practice
C	Overfishing: Causes, effects and possible solutions
D	Urban and peri-urban forestry for sustainable urban development
E	Ecology in Times of Scarcity
F	Critical thinking: Definitions, assessment and implementation

Unit summary

1   **Answers:**
a. F
b. F
c. T
d. F
e. T

2   Answers depend on students, but some ideas are:
- questions about feedback from a previous assignment
- updating your tutor on your progress on independent projects
- clarifying points from the course materials / lectures that you don't understand
- asking for advice about where to find information

3   **Possible answers:**
a. The meaning of the Latin word that plagiarism comes from is *thief.*
b. If you plagiarize, you are stealing someone's ideas.
c. Answers depend on students – one of the most common reasons is that they don't know it is wrong to copy ideas. Also, they may find it difficult to understand what they are reading and write it in their own words.
d. Some of the possible consequences of plagiarizing are being expelled from a university and harming one's career prospects.

Possible answers:

1. Find something in your subject area you are interested in.
2. Look for sources.
3. Decide how much you already know about the topic.
4. Decide how practical it is to work on this topic.
5. Talk about your ideas.
6. Think about a possible working title.
7. Summarize your project idea in one sentence.
8. Make a plan.

It's important to emphasize here the importance of considering the intended audience for any writing that students do.

| Task 2 | Developing a topic |

2.1 **Answers:**

Most general ➔	← General/specific ➔	← Most specific
4, 7, 9	2, 6	1, 3, 5, 8

As a whole-class activity, you could ask the students to explain why each title belongs in each column.

| Task 3 | Establishing a focus |

3.1 This activity will work well if you arrange the students initially in groups or pairs. They should attempt to form questions together. Then get one group of students to present their questions and ask for further suggestions from the rest of the class. The questions below could be distributed to students for them to compare with their own (as a checklist and a basis for discussion).

Example questions:

- What problems exist in the Argentinian education system?
- How can the Argentinian education system be improved?
- Which countries have a similar education system to Argentina?
- What attempts at improvement have already been made?
- What specific challenges do policymakers/teachers/students face in Argentina?

3.2 This task again lends itself to pair or group work and could be carried out in the same way as Ex 3.1. You could ask each pair or group to look at two or three of the titles and make suggestions before sharing their ideas with the rest of the class.

Note that the suggested answers are available as a photocopiable handout in Appendix 5a on pages 61–62.

Task 4 — Establishing a working title

The aim of this task is to show students how working titles are flexible and developmental. It also gives them training in developing titles that are more specific and more academic in style.

4.1 Ask the students to look at the titles and decide if they agree that the student has moved from a more general focus to a more specific one.

4.2 Copy the titles and get students to compare their ideas about how the titles could be made more specific before showing them the sample answers, which are available as a photocopiable handout in Appendix 5b on page 63. Explain that these are all authentic examples of titles used by pre-sessional students.

4.3 This will probably be most effective if set initially as a homework task so that students can go to the library or search the Internet independently. Foundation or undergraduate students may need more support with this task than postgraduates. Students should be encouraged to spend time planning and working out their ideas.

Ask them to share their working titles in groups, giving each other feedback on how general or specific they are and asking questions that might help them to further focus their ideas.

Task 5 — Planning Project 2

5.1 As noted, students often find it difficult to establish a focus for their project. The questions in the Project plan act as guidelines to help them do so.

Encourage the students to complete the plan as far as possible. This will probably need to be done as a homework task because students will need time to reflect.

In the following lesson, a brief class discussion should help students who have been unable to complete their planning for homework. This will also give students the opportunity to verbalize their ideas and thus clarify them.

Some model notes are available to students as a photocopiable handout in Appendix 5c on page 64, or they can be projected on an OHP or other visual medium for general discussion or for one-to-one tutorial work with students who are experiencing difficulty in formulating a plan.

Unit summary

1 **Answers:**
a. 2 or 6
b. 1 or 3
c. 5
d. 4
e. 3

2

Answers:

Answers depend on students, but these are some possible pieces of advice.

a. Because a topic that is too general lacks focus. / Because you will be able to explore a topic in more depth.

b. You can ask specific questions and narrow down the range. / You can rewrite the working title so that it is more specific.

3

Answers:

a. establish a focus

b. frequently

c. being general to being specific

4

Answers:

Answers depend on students. You could ask the students to share their answers to this in small groups.

Appendix 5a

Examples of finding a specific focus for general topics

Milk supply and production
- How important is milk as part of the human diet?
- Where is milk most widely produced?
- Is cow's milk more or less good for you than, for example, goat's milk?
- What factors make milk an important dietary requirement?
- Are there substitutes for milk?
- Does milk have any properties likely to cause allergies in humans? If so, what are the most significant examples?

Demographic trends
- What are the most prevalent current global demographic trends?
- Are any measures being taken to control trends?
- Is it actually necessary for measures to be taken?

Intelligent buildings
- What is an *intelligent building*?
- What is the benefit of intelligent buildings compared with other buildings?
- How do the costs compare with 'normal' buildings?
- How are intelligent buildings likely to feature in future town and city planning? (this could refer to a specific country, city or town)

The United Nations
- What is the role of the United Nations?
- How effective is it in carrying out this role?
- In what areas has the work of the United Nations been most successful?

Genetically modified (GM) food
- How safe is GM food?
- Why is food being genetically modified?
- How is food genetically modified?
- What are the advantages of genetically modified food?
- Why are many people resistant to GM modification?

China's construction industry
- How big is China's construction industry?
- What factors have led to its expansion?
- Has there been one particular factor, such as the Beijing Olympics, which has been particularly significant?
- Is the structure of the industry similar to that in other countries?
- What socio-economic impact has the expansion had on China?
- Have there been any significant global impacts?

PHOTOCOPIABLE

Class size
- In what context is class size important?
- How relevant is class size to effective learning?
- Has research been carried out on the impact of class size on learning?
- What aspects of learning are affected by class size?

Vitamin C and the common cold
- Does taking vitamin C really help counteract the common cold?
- Is a cure likely to be found for the common cold?
- What are the natural sources of vitamin C?
- Does vitamin C combine effectively with other common cold medications?
- What has research revealed on the effectiveness of vitamin C as a means of either preventing or helping cure the common cold?

Branding
- What is *branding*?
- How important is it in terms of sales?
- Is branding the single most important factor in selling? If not, what is?
- What particular brand names have had a global impact?
- What are the most effective means of branding?

Future developments in human health
- To what extent does the discovery of new cures or methods of treatment impact on global health?
- Are there factors other than new treatments and medical care to be considered for the future?
- What new diseases are resulting from living in the 21st century? If so, what are they?
- What major developments have been made in the last 100 years in improving human health?

PHOTOCOPIABLE

Appendix 5b

Rewriting essay titles

1. Learning a second language
⬇

Motivation is key in learning a second language
⬇

Although a number of factors are involved in successfully learning a second language, motivation is the most important factor

2. Organic food and health
⬇

Eating organic food has a positive impact on human health
⬇

People who eat organic food have healthier organs

3. The effect of technology on society
⬇

The general impact of technology on education
⬇

The positive impact of technological development on teaching methodology

PHOTOCOPIABLE

Planning Project 2: Model notes

What is your topic?

The role of the family in 21st-century Turkey.

Why have you chosen this topic?

- The academic subject is sociology.
- The role of the family is changing in Turkey (effects of globalization & transition from traditional model to 21st-century model).
- The impact on society is significant.

Key questions (what do you want to find out about this topic?)

- Should the traditional role of the family in Turkey be retained?
- What are these 'traditional family values'?
- What are the positive and negative effects of retaining traditional family values/adopting modern family values?

What is your focus and/or working title?

In what way is the role of the traditional family having an impact on modern Turkish society?

Thesis statement

The changing role of the Turkish family is having a negative impact on social values. Change is inevitable, but the rate of change is making the negative aspects difficult to control.

Specific title

The problems associated with the changing role of the Turkish family need to be urgently addressed for the 21st century.

PHOTOCOPIABLE

6 Introductions, conclusions and definitions

In this unit students will:

- analyze the features of introductions
- analyze the features of conclusions
- analyze the features of definitions
- identify the language of each of these three components in a typical academic text

Introduction

The purpose of this unit is to get students to look at certain aspects of their project.

INPUT Writing introductions

Before the students read the Input box here, you may like to ask them what they know about introductions and conclusions already and write up their ideas on the board. They can then read the Input text to check if it mentions anything they hadn't thought of. Then these ideas can also be added to the list on the board.

If your students are using *EAS: Writing*, they will be able to use the microskills they have been developing on that course as well as their experience of writing their project so far, including feedback. If students have written an introduction, ask them to bring a hard copy to class for Task 2. (Alternatively, they could bring a copy of the introduction to a previous project they have written.)

Ask students what they already know about the features of introductions before you look at page 74 of the Course Book. In small groups, get them to discuss the purpose of introductions. They may have covered this in *EAS: Writing*. After eliciting ideas (students should produce most of those on the list in the Course Book), look at the features on page 74 of the Course Book and explain Ex 1.1.

Task 1 Features of introductions

1.1 Students should look at Introduction 1 and consider which of the features listed in the Input box can be found here. This exercise can be discussed as a whole class. Emphasize that introductions may only have some of the features listed in the Input box, depending on the writer's purpose.

1.2 The students can check their ideas from Ex 1.1 with the notes in the table here.

It will be clear from this example that certain features overlap. For example, background information may be considered in part as justification, and the thesis statement may be linked with the writer's purpose. Furthermore, certain features are not always included. For example, in this introduction, there is no definition or outline of what is to follow in the text.

It may be worth pointing out here that it is generally a good idea to try to include an outline of what is to come, as this helps to set the context for the reader and also for, students to check that their ideas are clearly organized.

1.3 This and the following exercises are designed to encourage students to analyze the features of introductions and compare ways in which they are written. They do this with decreasing amounts of scaffolding and prompts.

Group work and reporting back

You may prefer to put the students into small groups and assign one or two of the introductions (2–5). They should analyze their introduction and then report back to the rest of the class on the features they identified and examples of these.

The following introduction tables are also available as photocopiable handouts in Appendix 6a on pages 75–79, so they can be projected on an OHP (or other visual medium).

Answer:

Introduction 2: *What role does the real estate property market play in the economy?*

Feature	Relevant section of text
introduction to topic	(a) The real estate property market plays an essential role in the economic system of any country. On average, property accounts for 60% of national wealth (Walker & Flanagan, 1991).
background information	(b) <u>Broadly speaking</u>, the real estate market involves many industries, including construction, commerce, retail and services, thus acting as an economic focus point.
justification	(c) <u>This essay aims to show that</u> even though the real estate market plays a similar role in different countries, it does in fact have a different impact on economies at different stages of maturity: for example, the different impact on developed and developing countries.
outline of structure	(d) Two countries <u>are compared in order to</u> identify these differences: the USA as a developed country, and China as a developing country. It gives some background to the real estate market: specifically property and capital. Secondly, it describes the role real estate plays in the economy, and finally it evaluates the key differences, showing that – in developing countries – the real estate market promotes the national economy through industry, and in developed countries this is done through the capital market.
definition of key terms	Not included.
thesis statement	Not included.
writer's purpose	Same as *justification* in row 3 above.

1.4   **Answer:**

Introduction 3: *A discussion of how green buildings can be both environmentally friendly and a profitable venture*

Feature	Relevant section of text
introduction to topic	(lines 1–6) Most human activities occur within a building. This is where we live, work, produce goods and products, and entertain. At the same time, the function of any 'construction', from the time of primitive caves, has been to protect people from the hazards of their surroundings. Nevertheless, the environment has suffered serious damage caused by buildings, due to their reliance on energy production and the amount of waste water that is generated.
background information	(lines 7–13) <u>With recent discussion about</u> the importance of the environment and climate change, society has begun to show concern about how its habits and processes might be modified in order to have less impact on nature. In civil engineering, this view – combined mainly with the increase of energy prices – has led to the advent of <u>green buildings</u> (BAHBA, 1994). Those who construct or manage buildings – the real estate investors – are faced with the challenge of seeking a solution to reduce the costs of construction and maintenance. (lines 23–25) In other sectors of construction, where green buildings are not yet significant, they are not as costly a solution for reducing the impact of houses on the environment as is often believed.
justification	(lines 26–29) <u>The aim of this essay is to show how</u> buildings cause damage to the environment, emphasizing the issues of energy and water supply, and discussing the extent to which green buildings can mitigate these problems whilst still being profitable ventures for investors.
outline of structure	Not included.
definition of key terms	Not included.
thesis statement	(lines 14–25) As far as investment in the real estate market is concerned, investors are especially interested in projects with the highest yield, which sometimes means that the initial investment, namely the construction of the building, might be low. However, as green building techniques are currently not widely used, the construction of a green building generally requires a greater amount of initial funding than for traditional buildings. Despite the cost factor, the United States Green Building Council (USGBC, 2009) indicates that the construction of these ventures is rapidly increasing in the USA; from 2% on non-residential buildings in 2005 to 10% in 2008, and predicted to be 20% in 2013. In other sectors of construction, where green buildings are not yet significant, they are not as costly a solution for reducing the impact of houses on the environment as is often believed.
writer's purpose	Same as *justification* in row 3 above.

Answers:

Introduction 4: *Developing customer loyalty: Current strategies and their effectiveness*

Feature	Relevant section of text
introduction to topic	(lines 1–5) Nowadays, as companies compete with each other for survival, there are a number of factors which influence every market. These include customer care, which is one of the best ways to guarantee the future of a company. Customer care represents long-term investment and generates income. Satisfied customers are more likely to repeat their purchases.
background information	Not included.
justification	(lines 5–6) For this reason, understanding their behaviour is the key to survival.
outline of structure	(lines 13–16) This essay analyzes the different types of loyalty and discusses the extent to which the main approaches that are used by companies to gain customer loyalty are actually effective.
definition of key terms	(lines 6–11) To this end, different companies have experimented with new methods in order to build a strong customer relationship. These can be categorized as indirect and direct methods, depending on the kind of marketing they involve. The former focuses on maintaining the corporate image, whilst the latter emphasizes the product.
thesis statement	(lines 11–13) Even though both methods have the same goal of extended loyalty, recent research shows that direct methods seem to lead to different ends, probably due to the nature of this specific methodology.
writer's purpose	Same as *justification* in row 3 above.

Introduction 5: *The problem of overfishing in the great lakes of developing African countries and a review of current policy*

Feature	Relevant section of text
introduction to topic	(lines 1–8) Over the past decades, overfishing has been identified as one of the main threats to the sustainability of aquatic ecosystems, although policies to regulate it are in place. The current policy implemented by developing African countries with great lakes, such as Zambia and Tanzania, addresses the conservation and sustainable use of fisheries' resources, but has not been successful in addressing the problem of the depletion of these resources. This is because the policy emphasizes resource conservation rather than alternatives that would remedy the situation.

background information	(lines 14–19) <u>This implies that</u> when a particular species is overfished, either for food or commercial purposes, there is a problem. This is experienced when most of the fishing community in developing African countries depend on fishing as one of their major socio-economic activities and overfishing can lead to loss of employment, income and sources of food. (lines 20–22) Fish numbers taken from lakes have undoubtedly increased at an alarming rate over the past 10–15 years, and this threatens the availability of some varieties.
justification	(lines 8–11) <u>Hence, the policy needs to be reviewed in order to</u> incorporate measures that would have a positive impact and reduce the depletion of resources that has caused an overfishing problem in the lakes.
outline of structure	(lines 23–27) <u>This essay will give an overview of the overfishing problem and explain how it happens. It will attempt to identify</u> the people responsible for this problem, evaluate the current policy on overfishing and recommend how the problem can be reduced.
definition of key terms	(lines 12–14) <u>The term overfishing can be defined as</u> the 'exploitation of the resource beyond the maximum sustainable yield (MSY) as a result of over-intensive fishing as the stock biomass is decreasing' (Travers et al., 2010).
thesis statement	(lines 22–23) A policy with a precautionary approach would reduce the overfishing problems and improve the fishery resource stock.
writer's purpose	Same as *justification* in row 3 above.

Task 2   Analyzing your introduction

2.1 – 2.3   Answers will depend on students. Be prepared to discuss any extra features students may find in their introductions. If they are not in the list of features discussed above, they should probably feature later in the essay, rather than in the introduction.

Students should also be wary of providing too much general background information. It may also be a good time now to point out that introductions generally move from general to specific ideas, setting the context and then narrowing the focus to explain what will be covered in that particular text.

Task 3   The language of introductions

3.1/ 3.2   In this task, students are asked to look at Introductions 1–5 again, and to identify typical expressions used in introductions. Answers are underlined in the introduction texts in the notes for Ex 1.3–1.5, and photocopiable handouts of the notes are also available in Appendix 6a on pages 75–79.

Constant reinforcement of the language development of the students is essential, and one way of doing this is to continually raise awareness of language. Exposure to these expressions in context (rather than as isolated pieces of language) is important. Encourage discussion of the phrases that students identify, and urge them to use this language in their own work, writing out some example sentences they might find useful in Ex 3.2.

| Task 4 | Identifying the thesis statement |

This task gives students more practice in identifying and writing strong thesis statements. It will probably help the students if you emphasize that a thesis statement tells the reader what the writer's viewpoint or stance on the topic is.

4.1 **Answers:**

1. The cocoa bean contains many nutrients, from fat to vitamin C, as well as caffeine. <u>B</u>
2. Although excessive amounts of caffeine can be damaging to health, recent research indicates that a limited amount can be beneficial. <u>T</u>
3. It stimulates the brain, aids concentration and may help to limit the effects of certain diseases such as Alzheimer's and Parkinson's. <u>E</u>

4.2 This is a good example of where a thesis statement is not always obvious and is open for discussion. A brief discussion on this text should encourage students to engage in critical evaluation.

It is worth explaining here that it is better to have a clearly stated thesis statement as it enables the reader to more easily follow the writer's argument and viewpoint through the text.

Answers:

1. '<u>However, at certain periods fundamentally different processes of urbanisation have emerged. The result has been that the rate of urban change has accelerated and new, distinctly different, urban forms have developed</u>'. This is because the following text will clearly attempt to demonstrate/prove this fact and show how the processes of urbanization are, in fact, 'fundamentally different'.

    This is, therefore, not a thesis statement of intent, but rather a hypothesis which the author sets out to prove. It may suggest an element of textual organization, i.e., a description/exemplification of urban changes followed by discussion to 'prove' the hypothesis. This is a fairly logical assumption of the likely organization.

2. Sentence 1: background information

    Sentence 2: background information

    Sentence 3: explanation

    Sentence 4: explanation

    Sentence 5: thesis statement

    Sentence 6: thesis statement

    Sentence 7: example (this supports the thesis statement made in sentences 5 and 6)

4.3/ 4.4 You may wish to present the model answer on the photocopiable handout in Appendix 6b on page 80 to students after they have completed Ex 4.3, for comparison. It is worth pointing out that very often the thesis statement may be implied rather than explicitly stated. In the model answer, however, the thesis statement (underlined) is extended over two sentences.

After looking at the model answer, it is worth asking students what they think the implications might be, e.g., over-reliance on technology, less effort to learn and memorize (is this good or bad?), the need to develop greater critical awareness to compensate for the lost effort of memory retention, etc.

| Task 5 | **Features of conclusions** |

You may prefer to work on this whole section (Tasks 5–7) at a different time if your students are not yet at the stage of writing their own conclusions.

INPUT Writing conclusions
As with the work on introductions, first elicit what the students know about the typical features of a conclusion, then direct them to the list in the Course Book.

5.1   With a lower-level group, you could work through the features of the example conclusion.

Answer:

Feature	Relevant section of text
logical conclusion	Although there are a number of methods in capital markets for raising funds, borrowing from banks seems to be the best choice for small and medium-sized enterprises that want to expand.
brief summary	This project has examined how the development of small and medium-sized businesses in the economic sector partly depends on financial management and financial decisions when choosing a suitable method to raise funds are crucial. The importance of a clear financial plan, understanding financial situations, and clarifying the advantages and disadvantages of each method has been discussed.
comments on ideas	(... this essay has shown how bank borrowing is suitable for the business environment in Vietnam.) This is because many businesses are family-run, with a lack of management experience, but also because interest charges are deductible for such companies. The same lack of experience would make it difficult to venture into new capital markets, and currently, at least, bank loans are the most appropriate source of funding.
predictions	As experience grows, however, and the depth of knowledge increases, it is important for these companies to consider other possible financial options.
further research suggestions	Not included.
limitations	Not included.
reference to thesis	... this essay has shown how bank borrowing is suitable for the business environment in Vietnam.

5.2/ 5.3 As with the exercises in the task on introductions, it may work better to assign one conclusion to groups of students, ask them to analyze it and then regroup to discuss answers as a whole class.

Answers:

The answers for this task are given as photocopiable handouts in Appendix 6c on pages 81–82.

5.4 **Answers:**

Feature	Conclusion 1	Conclusion 2	Conclusion 3	Conclusion 4
logical conclusion		✔	✔	
brief summary	✔	✔	✔	✔
comments on ideas	✔	✔	✔	✔
predictions	✔	✔		✔
further research suggestions				
limitations		✔		
reference to thesis statement	✔	✔	✔	✔

Task 6	Analyzing your conclusion

6.1 – 6.3 Leave this task until students have completed the conclusions to their projects. Be prepared to discuss any extra features students might find in their conclusions. If these are not in the list of features discussed above, they could be included in an earlier section of the essay.

Task 7	The language of conclusions

7.1 You may also like to ask the students to write the phrases in groups according to the function that they have, e.g., phrases for introducing contrasting points, phrases for introducing predictions, etc.

Answers:

Examples of useful academic phrases which could be used are underlined on the photocopiable handouts in Appendix 6c on pages 81–82.

Note: Conclusion 2 contains use of the passive voice and cautious language.

Study skills: Recording useful phrases

It might be a good idea to encourage the students to keep a notebook specifically for useful phrases that they come across and may want to use in their own writing.

As suggested earlier, these phrases could be grouped together according to their function. Students could also experiment with creating a mind map of these phrases, adding to it as they go through the course and their period of academic study.

It would be worth noting that they should try to record an example of the phrase in use, not just individual words, to show how it is used in context.

Task 8	Features of definitions

Definitions have different features depending on their usage. As with introductions and conclusions, it is worthwhile eliciting what is already known about definitions. For example, it could be said that a definition is a statement about what a word means depending on whether or not it is a 'dictionary' definition – that is, an expert and widely accepted definition. An expert in this case might be an academic, or equally an expert in a specific field, an author, etc. There are also personal definitions.

INPUT Writing Extended Definitions (1)

Highlight how important it is to establish the definition(s) of key term(s). Students should also consider who the reader is and the purpose of their writing. Students need to understand the key terms themselves first, before they can demonstrate their understanding of them to their tutors. It is worth pointing out that academic writing often defines key terms to establish the precise interpretation of these terms and to avoid any scope for misunderstanding.

8.1 It is worth highlighting here the point about considering the audience the writing is intended for when making decisions about which terms to define and in how much detail.

8.2 As before, depending on the level of the group and how much practice you feel they need, you may want to ask the students to work in pairs or individually through all the definitions, or assign one definition to analyze to each group of students, before asking them to share their ideas as a class.

Note: Make sure that it is understood that 'expansion' could refer to exemplification or explanation.

Answers:

These are given as photocopiable handouts in Appendix 6d on pages 83–84.

8.3 **Answer:**

Feature	1	2	3	4
a formal definition, e.g., from a dictionary or an expert in the field	✔	✔	✔	✔
an expansion of the definition with an explanation and/or examples	✔	✔	✔	✔
a comment on the definition by the writer	✔	✔	✔	✔
references	✔	✔	✔	✔

8.4 Useful phrases are given in italics in the definitions on the photocopiable handouts in Appendices 6a–6d on pages 75–84.

8.5 The most useful definition might be Definition 2, because background information about the evolution of the term *critical thinking* leads to a precise and widely accepted definition of the term.

The choice, however, is open to discussion, and this should be encouraged.

INPUT Writing Extended Definitions (2)

When writing for academic purposes, it is better that students avoid using a general English dictionary and use either a subject-specific dictionary or a direct quotation or paraphrase of experts in the field. It is important to remind students that when using the definitions of other writers/experts in their own essays, they will need to make clear whether or not they agree or disagree with the expert's attitude towards the term.

8.6 Remind students that their definition is intended for the 'educated' reader and needs to be expressed appropriately using relatively formal language. However, it needs to be clear and concise so that a non-specialist will be able to understand it.

Unit summary

1
Answers:
a. FI
b. FC
c. FI
d. FC
e. FC
f. FI
g. FI
h. FC
i. FI
j. FI
k. FC

2
Answers:
Answers depend on students, but it would be worth checking them with the students, perhaps in one-to-one tutorials if you do these.

3
Answers:
When writing about a topic, you must clarify your <u>terms</u> (explain clearly what you mean by any key words you use) so that the writer and the reader have the same <u>interpretation</u>. If you are new to the subject, you will need to define the most basic terms so that you understand them properly. As you gain <u>knowledge</u> of the subject, and if you are writing for specialists, the meaning of certain key terms can be assumed as part of <u>shared knowledge</u>. You can use formal definitions from a <u>dictionary</u> or an expert in the field, expand a definition with explanations or <u>examples</u>, or make a <u>comment</u> about the definition.

Appendix 6a

Introduction 1: *To what extent is bank borrowing the best choice for small and medium-sized enterprises raising funds in Vietnam?*

Feature	Relevant section of text
introduction to topic	*In the economic development process in Vietnam, small and medium-sized enterprises are increasingly encouraged to expand.*
background information	*<u>In promoting the growth of these companies</u>, raising capital plays an important role in improving and marketing new products, expanding industries and managing daily operations.*
justification	*<u>According to</u> the World Bank's reports, companies can raise money from several sources: from capital markets, from buying and selling shares, owning the franchise or increasing venture capital (2006).* *<u>Another common alternative</u> is bank borrowing.*
outline of structure	Not included.
definition of key terms	Not included.
thesis statement	*Borrowing from the bank appears to be particularly convenient for small firms in developing economies.*
writer's purpose	*<u>By examining</u> the features of bank borrowing, this paper will show that this is the best choice for Vietnamese small enterprises.*

PHOTOCOPIABLE

Introduction 2: *What role does the real estate property market play in the economy?*

Feature	Relevant section of text
introduction to topic	(a) The real estate property market plays an essential role in the economic system of any country. On average, property accounts for 60% of national wealth (Walker & Flanagan, 1991).
background information	(b) <u>Broadly speaking</u>, the real estate market involves many industries, including construction, commerce, retail and services, thus acting as an economic focus point.
justification	(c) <u>This essay aims to show that</u> even though the real estate market plays a similar role in different countries, it does in fact have a different impact on economies at different stages of maturity: for example, the different impact on developed and developing countries.
outline of structure	(d) Two countries <u>are compared in order to</u> identify these differences: the USA as a developed country, and China as a developing country. It gives some background to the real estate market: specifically property and capital. Secondly, it describes the role real estate plays in the economy, and finally it evaluates the key differences, showing that – in developing countries – the real estate market promotes the national economy through industry, and in developed countries this is done through the capital market.
definition of key terms	Not included.
thesis statement	Not included.
writer's purpose	Same as *justification* in row 3 above.

Introduction 3: *A discussion of how green buildings can be both environmentally friendly and a profitable venture*

Feature	Relevant section of text
introduction to topic	(lines 1–6) Most human activities occur within a building. This is where we live, work, produce goods and products, and entertain. At the same time, the function of any 'construction', from the time of primitive caves, has been to protect people from the hazards of their surroundings. Nevertheless, the environment has suffered serious damage caused by buildings, due to their reliance on energy production and the amount of waste water that is generated.
background information	(lines 7–13) <u>With recent discussion about</u> the importance of the environment and climate change, society has begun to show concern about how its habits and processes might be modified in order to have less impact on nature. In civil engineering, this view – combined mainly with the increase of energy prices – has led to the advent of *green buildings* (BAHBA, 1994). Those who construct or manage buildings – the real estate investors – are faced with the challenge of seeking a solution to reduce the costs of construction and maintenance. (lines 23–25) In other sectors of construction, where green buildings are not yet significant, they are not as costly a solution for reducing the impact of houses on the environment as is often believed.
justification	(lines 26–29) <u>The aim of this essay is to show how</u> buildings cause damage to the environment, emphasizing the issues of energy and water supply, and discussing the extent to which green buildings can mitigate these problems whilst still being profitable ventures for investors.
outline of structure	Not included.
definition of key terms	Not included.
thesis statement	(lines 14–25) As far as investment in the real estate market is concerned, investors are especially interested in projects with the highest yield, which sometimes means that the initial investment, namely the construction of the building, might be low. However, as green building techniques are currently not widely used, the construction of a green building generally requires a greater amount of initial funding than for traditional buildings. Despite the cost factor, the United States Green Building Council (USGBC, 2009) indicates that the construction of these ventures is rapidly increasing in the USA; from 2% on non-residential buildings in 2005 to 10% in 2008, and predicted to be 20% in 2013. In other sectors of construction, where green buildings are not yet significant, they are not as costly a solution for reducing the impact of houses on the environment as is often believed.
writer's purpose	Same as *justification* in row 3 above.

PHOTOCOPIABLE

Writing an introduction with a thesis statement

Model answer:

The onset of the 21ˢᵗ century has seen the full awakening of the age of requesting/accessing 'digital' information. Such knowledge-seeking is manifested variously through powerful search engines or global positioning systems (satellite navigation); the verb 'google' has become synonymous with the idea of locating information. <u>There is, however, a growing concern that anyone seeking information in this way is handing over responsibility for 'knowing geography' or, in fact, outsourcing the task to the Internet for any access to general knowledge. The danger, it would appear, is that the concept of retaining knowledge in one's head is gradually becoming outmoded.</u> This text will look at some of the implications of digital knowledge-seeking, and will suggest possible short- and longer-term outcomes.

PHOTOCOPIABLE

Appendix 6c

Identifying features of conclusions

Key: 1 further research suggestions; **2** limitations; **3** comments on ideas; **4** logical conclusion; **5** predictions; **6** brief summary; **7** reference to thesis statement

Conclusion 1: *What role does the real estate property market play in the economy?*

6 <u>*This essay has shown that*</u> *the real estate market has different functions depending on whether the country involved has either a developing or developed economy.* <u>*In general,*</u> *real estate property is a national asset, and the real estate market is indispensable for national economic development. In China, where the real estate market is immature but growing rapidly, the national economy is more dependent on this market with its potential for employment, and possibility of attracting capital.* <u>*In this situation,*</u> *and ultimately as the Chinese government is the largest investor, the real estate market can be considered the engine of change.* <u>*In contrast,*</u> *the real estate market in the USA is mature, involved in many sections of the economy, and individuals are the largest investors.* **3/5** <u>*It remains to be seen whether*</u> *the development of the Chinese economy will have a significant impact on the real estate market, creating a situation more similar to that of the American model.*

Conclusion 2: *A discussion of how green buildings can be both environmentally friendly and a profitable venture*

6 *Ways of decreasing the impact of construction on the environment* <u>*have been analyzed,*</u> *and the way in which these solutions can result,* <u>*to some extent,*</u> *in higher profits for their investors* <u>*has been explained.*</u> **4/7** <u>*It is suggested that*</u> *green buildings can create additional value for the investor, since they reduce maintenance costs and thus increase profitability.* **2** <u>*Although*</u> *only the use of solar energy for heating and light* <u>*has been analyzed,*</u> **6** <u>*it has been demonstrated*</u> *how this usage can diminish the impact of building activities on the environment, and increase the profits for investors.* **3** <u>*However,*</u> *this cannot be a global solution, since its effectiveness is restricted to sites with sufficient intense sunlight. In other areas, the re-use of 'grey' water and the harvesting of rainwater are alternative environmentally friendly solutions even though the high cost of drinkable water decreases its feasibility as a profitable venture.* **5** <u>*Nonetheless,*</u> *should these techniques become widely used, and other cheaper solutions evolve, green buildings* <u>*might indeed*</u> *become both a totally environmentally friendly and profitable solution.*

PHOTOCOPIABLE

Conclusion 3: *Developing customer loyalty: Current strategies and their effectiveness*

6 *Customer loyalty is essential for the future of firms, and companies need to develop different marketing strategies in order to create long-term loyalty. Both indirect methods, which are concerned with the image of the company, and direct methods, which emphasize the product, goods or service, <u>are identified</u> as possible strategies. Although both methods work well <u>in theory</u>, <u>in practice</u> it is shown that indirect methods are more efficient, and can provide a deeper loyalty, mainly based on trust and customer care. <u>As indicated</u>, the IKEA model is evidence of how a trained staff member can retain a customer's loyalty, even in different cultural situations.*

2 *<u>In contrast</u>, direct methods often create 'false' loyalty, which may be useful only in the short term. <u>Furthermore</u>, building loyalty is not guaranteed with this approach, and sometimes there are huge drawbacks.* **3** *<u>Thus</u>, if the marketing plan is not well thought out and executed, companies may waste money in useless reward programmes. Many approaches used in recent years <u>have shown that</u> customers have individual personalities and gifts are not a sufficient general means of ensuring loyalty. <u>Even though</u> direct methods have some drawbacks, they can be useful, at least whilst the company is building a better image.* **7** *<u>For this reason</u>, a combination of both methods <u>might be a better option</u>.* **4** *<u>As Riechheld's research demonstrates</u>, the best way to guarantee a company's future is to build a better corporate and brand image which shows the strengths of the company, without gimmicks.*

Conclusion 4: *The problem of overfishing in the great lakes of developing African countries and a review of current policy*

7 *<u>This essay has shown that</u> in order to reduce or eliminate the overfishing problem in developing East African countries, current policy needs to be reviewed to include a precautionary approach in rectifying the drastic depletion of fishing stock.* **6** *<u>This approach should</u> address issues such as the stakeholders' future position if restrictions such as quota fishing and closed season fishing are imposed. <u>It would also be significantly more effective if</u> other alternatives for obtaining fish for local industry and personal consumption by the local community were considered.* **3** *<u>For example</u>, fish farming would be a good option as the commercial industry would still get raw fish material for the factories and hence continue to meet its fish market demand. This would also ensure that local communities could generate sufficient income for their needs.* **5** *<u>Eventually</u>, this approach would reduce the fishing pressure on inland waterways and eliminate the overfishing problem in the region.*

Appendix 6d

Identifying features of definitions

Key: 1 formal definition (from dictionary/expert); **2** expansion of definition; **3** comment on definition; **4** references

Definition 1: Language aptitude

Some people have a natural language ability, which makes them adept at learning foreign languages, whereas others are rather poor at this, and struggle to acquire a basic communicative ability in the language. A factor that makes a difference to the individual is often referred to as language aptitude. **1** *Although difficult to define in concrete terms, it is understood to be not necessarily the ability to learn the language in the classroom, but rather to be able to apply this knowledge in a real-life situation (Cook, 1991).* **2** *While some people argue that this ability is not fixed, Carroll (1981) believes that aptitude is an innate or stable factor, which cannot be changed through training and is constant throughout one's life. He also insists that it is not related to past learning experience. This implies that language aptitude is not something that is accumulated as we age, but something we are born with.* **3** *This may sound demotivating for those who are not equipped with language aptitude.* However, as Ellis (1994) suggests, aptitude is only a facilitator which encourages learning, especially in accelerating the rate of learning, but does not determine learning.
4 Cook (1991), Carroll (1981) and Ellis (1994)

Definition 2: Critical thinking

As the importance of critical thinking has become widely accepted, scholars and theorists have attempted <u>to establish a clear definition</u>. Critical thinking can be traced back more than 2,500 years to Socrates' time. **1** *Paul, Elder, and Bartell (1997) explained that it was <u>originally defined</u> as a method for arriving at the truth and analyzing complex ideas. This method of questioning, now known as 'Socratic questioning', is a series of questions about a certain issue used to investigate that issue by applying logical points of view.*

2 *However, the actual term 'critical thinking' only emerged in the 20th century. Renaud & Murray (2008) then assembled several popular definitions of critical thinking (e.g., Ennis, 1985; Furedy & Furedy, 1984; Pascarella & Terenzini, 2005; Watson & Glaser, 1980) which contain the following five common elements: identifying central issues and assumptions, making correct inferences from data, deducting conclusions from data provided, interpreting whether conclusions are warranted, and evaluating evidence or authority. <u>Other elements</u> of critical thinking <u>include</u>: making a statement or argument supported with evidence (Beyer, 1987), recognizing important relationships (Ennis, 1985; Furedy & Furedy, 1984; Pascarella and Terenzini, 2005), defining a problem (Dressel & Mayhew, 1954; Ennis, 1985), and forming relevant hypotheses (Dressel & Mayhew, 1954; Ennis, 1985).*

Despite this range, <u>one of the definitions of</u> critical thinking which is extensively accepted and <u>frequently cited</u> in academic works comes from the work of Michael Scriven and Richard Paul.

1 *Critical thinking is the intellectually disciplined process of actively and skilfully conceptualizing, applying, analyzing, synthesizing, and/or evaluating information gathered from, or generated by, observation, experience, reflection, reasoning, or communication, as a guide to belief and action. (Scriven & Paul, 1987, p. 5)*

PHOTOCOPIABLE

After this came a research project with the purpose of gaining consensus among 46 specialists from various disciplines who participated. The result was the Delphi Report, which emphasized that critical thinking was:

1 ... *purposeful, self-regulatory judgment which results in interpretation, analysis, evaluation, and inference, as well as explanation of evidential, conceptual, methodological, criteriological, or contextual considerations upon which that judgment is based. (Facione, 2010, p. 22)*

3 *This final definition is the basis of a number of education models which will be discussed in this paper's analysis of critical thinking.*

4 References given throughout definition (**1**) and expansion (**2**).

Definition 3: A green building

3 *Before defining the concept of green buildings, it is important to explain that although both constructions share some similarities, there are some misunderstandings about the differences between 'intelligent' buildings and 'green' buildings.* **1** *Ehrlich (2007)* <u>*conceptualizes*</u> *intelligent buildings as structures that use technologies and processes in order to increase productivity, efficiency and security in a building.* **3/2** <u>*The main purpose of*</u> *a green building, on the other hand, is for it to be built in a way that is 'friendly' to the environment, i.e., doesn't involve damaging it, and, as far as possible, uses sustainable resources.* **2** *Green buildings also use technologies based on natural processes, with the purpose of reducing the dependence on or use of resources, and consequently pollution.*

4 Ehrlich (2007)

Definition 4: Brand loyalty

3 <u>*A simple definition of*</u> *brand loyalty is not easy to produce because the loyalty idea does not just depend on one factor, but is instead a combination of factors that enlist the trust of customers in products and services.* **1** *Brand loyalty is simply derived from the word 'brand', but it is bonded through the company trademark and trustworthiness certification to encourage 'loyalty'. Trust is built on a long-term relationship between customers and companies that provide preferential services and products for customers (Larry, 1994).* **2** <u>*The three main factors involved in*</u> *brand loyalty are customer satisfaction, customer rewards and customer retention (Pallister & Law, 2007). However, no one factor can generate loyalty on its own.*

4 Larry (1994); Pallister & Law (2007)

Incorporating data and illustrations

In this unit students will:

- learn how data are incorporated into academic texts
- learn how to analyze data
- practise using the language of data commentary

Introduction

Before students begin Task 1, you could try to elicit the ideas outlined below, either with a brainstorming session in small groups or as a whole-class activity.

What are data? What is the purpose of data? What is the purpose of using pictures or diagrams? Why and when should students use data or illustrations in their projects?

Students can then use the results of the brainstorming to help them with the tasks in this unit.

Task 1	The purpose of data

1.1   **Possible answers:**

1. Data is information in the form of facts or statistics that can be analyzed.
2. Emphasize the fact that data can serve a number of purposes. Elicit these and list them on the board, if appropriate. Examples include:
   - to summarize information concisely
   - to clarify an idea or argument (make it more understandable)
   - to provide a source of evidence to support claims made in the text
   - to show the results of experiments or other forms of research, such as the results of questionnaires that a researcher has distributed
   - to give weight to an argument or hypothesis

It is important to emphasize that data or illustrations should only be included if they have a purpose. There is a tendency for students to include data or illustrations in their projects haphazardly, either as a result of anxiety or because they have seen other students include data in their own work. It is an aspect of a student's work that could be discussed during a one-to-one tutorial (the tutor may ask *Why have you included this table here?*).

Students should consider the actual positioning of any data they include in their work. The data material must be located as close as possible to the relevant reference to it in the text. Sometimes it is more appropriate to include certain data in the form of an appendix; if so, this must be cross-referenced in the text.

Examples of why data or illustrations might be included in an appendix rather than the main body of the text can also be discussed; e.g.,:

- size of a graphic (e.g., a map of the world)
- number of items (if there are too many tables and graphs it may be difficult for the reader to follow the text)
- requirements of a particular university department or subject area

2.1 Depending on the level of your class, you may want to give some input here before they begin this task on the differences between tables and figures.

Tables

Tables usually consist of listed information, e.g., a list of African cities with their comparative populations over three decades (for example, 1980, 1990 and 2000, set out in three columns). You could copy the following table onto the board as an example:

Table 1.1: Urban population growth in major African urban areas

City	1980	1990	2000
Cape Town	1.5m	2.3m	2.9m
Lusaka	1.0m	1.6m	2.8m

You may wish to point out that a caption that goes with tabulated data should go *above* the table, while a caption that accompanies a figure should go *below* the figure. It might help students if they remember the word *tabletop* in relation to this.

Figures

Figures can be charts, graphs, maps, photographs, diagrams, etc.

Answers:

Data 1 is a table. Data 2, 3 and 4 are figures.

2.2 Please note that data collected by organizations such as the Office for National Statistics shows data from the year previous to that given in the source information.

Answers:

1. *Household take-up of digital television by type of service* matches Data 3.
2. *Selected media activities that would be missed the most according to age, 2008* matches Data 4.

2.3 **Possible answers:**

Data 1: Readership of national daily newspapers
Data 2: Radio listening: by age, 2008

Remind students that for the table, the title should go at the top, but for the figure it goes underneath.

2.4 You may like to highlight the different ways that figures and tables can be referred to within a text. Students could brainstorm possible phrases in pairs and then discuss them as a class. Students will have further practice of referring to data in Task 5 of this unit. Some suggested phrases and ways of referring to the data are given in the answer below. This paragraph is also available as a photocopiable handout in Appendix 7a on page 90.

Possible answer:

In 2008, the 'digital switchover' began. Data from Ofcom (Figure 2) shows that nearly 87 per cent of homes in the UK had a digital television service at the end of the first quarter of 2008, a rise of 71 percentage points since 2000. A digital television set can also transmit digital radio stations. According to data from Radio Joint Audience Research Limited, shown here in Figure 1, the average time spent listening to the radio by people in the UK in the first quarter of 2007 was 19 hours and 24 minutes per week; average listening time increases with age. Between 2001–2002 and 2006–2007, radio listening fell among most age groups. <u>With reference to Table 1, it is clear that</u> the proportion of people reading a daily newspaper has also been declining for a number of years. The National Readership Survey shows that, on an average day, less than 44 per cent of people aged 15 and over in Great Britain read a national daily newspaper in the 12 months to June 2008, compared with 72 per cent in the 12 months to June 1978. In 2007, Ofcom asked which media activity respondents would miss the most if they were all taken away. <u>These results are illustrated in Figure 3.</u> Watching television would be the most missed activity for all age groups except those aged 16 to 19, who would miss the mobile phone the most.

Task 3	Assessing and interpreting data

3.1 Ask students to read the text and then compare how the data are presented and organized in Figure 1 on page 97 of the Course Book. They should then discuss how the information is encapsulated in the figure.

Possible answer:
The information given in the text matches that illustrated in the figure, e.g., *Would live and work for substantial period* cited in Figure 1 equates with the paragraph *The UK as a place to live* in the text. There are many more examples like this. The writer also provides some further comment on possible reasons for the results of the survey. The writer also makes some suggestions on how perceptions of Britain could be improved.

3.2 It may be a good idea to ask students to answer these questions in pairs or small groups, before checking answers as a whole class.

Possible answers:
1. The graph displays <u>information</u> showing how Britain is <u>perceived</u> by overseas visitors in various categories of life. This information is used to describe how Britain rates in each of these <u>areas</u> compared with 50 other <u>countries</u>.
2. educational opportunities; historic architecture; vibrant cities and contemporary culture; personal contacts within the UK
3. richness in natural beauty; welcoming visitors

3.3 **Possible answers:**
- Easy to distinguish between positive attractions and the less positive.
- Takes up much less space than the full text version and provides a useful checklist.
- Good use of colour to facilitate interpreting the content.

3.4 **Possible answer:**
Visitors, on the whole, apparently appreciate what Britain has to offer as a tourist destination and have generally positive perceptions.

Task 4	Working with data

4.1 **Answers:**
1. The main purpose of Figure 2 is to show the types of cultural products that people associate with the UK. This may be as a result of perception rather than direct experience.

2. Answers depend on students. It is perhaps most surprising that 20% of respondents did not associate any of these cultural products with the UK. It is not surprising that 50% of people associate museums with the UK, given the long history of the UK and the fact that many visitors are from countries with a shorter history.

3. The main conclusion we can draw from Figure 3 is that the most common perception of the UK is that it provides educational opportunities. This might be referring to museums and also to universities and opportunities for other academic studies.

4. These figures are bar charts.

4.2 It will probably work best to divide the students into groups to consider how they will conduct their mini-survey and collate the data. Depending on whether or not you have time, you may like to just ask the students to discuss how they would do this, rather than actually conduct the survey.

Some points to highlight are that as they are designing a questionnaire to compare their fellow students' ideas with those that are described in the figure, they will need to try to simulate the types of questions that they think the people originally surveyed may have answered.

They may also want to think about how they can best represent the data so that it is easy to make a comparison with the data from Figure 2. A bar chart with double lines for each area (in different colours) may work well.

4.3 **Answer:**

In 2009, hotels/guesthouses were the most <u>popular</u> type of paid accommodation for overseas visitors to the UK: <u>a quarter</u> stayed in this type of accommodation, <u>accounting for</u> 24% of all nights. There is <u>obviously</u> some visiting friends or relatives (VFR) crossover in the market, with <u>49%</u> of holiday visitors staying as a free guest with family or friends. Forty per cent of overseas visitors stayed as a free guest with friends or relatives, which <u>represented</u> 49% of all nights spent in the UK.

| Task 5 | **Incorporating references in a text** |

5.1 If you have not already done this in Ex 2.4, it would be a good idea to brainstorm and highlight key phrases and ways of incorporating references to figures and tables within a text. Further examples of this are given in the paragraph below. This paragraph is also reproduced as a photocopiable handout in Appendix 7b on page 91.

Possible answer:

Information has recently been released describing a variety of trends amongst visitors to Britain during 2000–2010. From the data, there is evidence of significant differences in how long overseas visitors tend to stay in Britain during a visit (Figure 6). Clearly, the VFR (visiting friends and relatives) sector is of some significance. This group tend to stay the greatest length of time, although up to 50% stay for free with friends or relatives <u>(Figure 4)</u>. As might be expected, there tend to be fluctuations in visitor numbers depending on the time of year. <u>This is illustrated in Figure 5.</u> Not surprisingly, the spring and summer periods attract the greatest number of visits. It is noticeable that these visits reach a peak during July–September. However, since the peak years of 2006–2007, there has been a steady decline in visitor numbers during all times of the year. In addition, the number of visitors who visit the UK from another country rather than their country of origin, or who visit a further country after their departure, is relatively small (<u>see Table 2</u>).

Unit summary

1 **Answers:**

Statement **d** is not true.

2–3 **Answers:**

Student answers will vary. Ask them to compare their ideas in pairs or small groups.

The digital switchover

In 2008, the 'digital switchover' began. Data from Ofcom (Figure 2) shows that nearly 87 per cent of homes in the UK had a digital television service at the end of the first quarter of 2008, a rise of 71 percentage points since 2000. A digital television set can also transmit digital radio stations. According to data from Radio Joint Audience Research Limited, shown here in Figure 1, the average time spent listening to the radio by people in the UK in the first quarter of 2007 was 19 hours and 24 minutes per week; average listening time increases with age. Between 2001–2002 and 2006–2007, radio listening fell among most age groups. With reference to Table 1, it is clear that the proportion of people reading a daily newspaper has also been declining for a number of years. The National Readership Survey shows that, on an average day, less than 44 per cent of people aged 15 and over in Great Britain read a national daily newspaper in the 12 months to June 2008, compared with 72 per cent in the 12 months to June 1978. In 2007, Ofcom asked which media activity respondents would miss the most if they were all taken away. These results are illustrated in Figure 3. Watching television would be the most missed activity for all age groups except those aged 16 to 19, who would miss the mobile phone the most.

Source: Adapted from Self, A. (Ed.). (2008). *Social trends 38* and Hughes, M. (Ed.). (2009). *Social trends 39*. Retrieved April 21, 2009, from National Statistics Online: www.statistics.gov.uk

Appendix 7b

Visitors to Britain

Information has recently been released describing a variety of trends amongst visitors to Britain during 2000–2010. From the data, there is evidence of significant differences in how long overseas visitors tend to stay in Britain during a visit (Figure 6). Clearly, the VFR (visiting friends and relatives) sector is of some significance. This group tend to stay the greatest length of time, although up to 50% stay for free with friends or relatives (Figure 4). As might be expected, there tend to be fluctuations in visitor numbers depending on the time of year. This is illustrated in Figure 5. Not surprisingly, the spring and summer periods attract the greatest number of visits. It is noticeable that these visits reach a peak during July–September. However, since the peak years of 2006–2007, there has been a steady decline in visitor numbers during all times of the year. In addition, the number of visitors who visit the UK from another country rather than their country of origin, or who visit a further country after their departure, is relatively small (see Table 2).

Source: Adapted from Visit Britain (2010). *Overseas visitors to Britain: Understanding Trends, Attitudes and Characteristics.* London: VisitBritain. Retrieved May 13, 2011, from www.visitbritain.org/Images/Overseas%20Visitors%20to%20Britain_tcm29-14708.pdf

PHOTOCOPIABLE

8 Preparing for conference presentations

In this unit students will:

- analyze, evaluate and practise writing abstracts
- prepare for an oral presentation using note cards and PowerPoint
- learn how to prepare a poster presentation
- edit the final draft of their projects

Introduction

In this unit, students will write two abstracts: one for their written project and one for a conference presentation. The abstract for the written project should be between 100 and 150 words in length.

Writing abstracts

Students have already been introduced to abstracts in Unit 4. Get them to read through the introduction to Unit 8 and then look back at Unit 4, as necessary.

Task 1   Identifying the features of abstracts

1.1   **Possible answers:**

Feature	1	2	3	4	5	6	7	8	9	10
Abstract 1	✔	✔	✔	✔		✔			✔	✔
Abstract 2	✔	✔	✔	✔	✔	✔		✔	✔	✔

Ask students to justify their answers and discuss as a class. Accept any reasonable answers.

1.2   Writing an abstract from memory is a useful way to focus on key points. Stress that students should write on the lines provided (this limits the length of their abstract).

1.3   After they have written their abstracts, students can exchange and peer-evaluate them, identifying the typical features of abstracts they discussed in Ex 1.1.

Task 2   Conference abstracts

2.1   **Answers:**

Abstract	Title
A	Mixed-use developments in the Kingdom of Saudi Arabia
B	Banking systems and management: Challenges facing Taiwanese banks

Abstract	Title
C	Interpretation and analysis of financial statements for non-accountants
D	Communication management in Transmission Control Protocol (TCP)
E	How the construction industry can contribute to the need to reduce energy consumption
F	Situation analysis in marketing
G	Foreign investment in China
H	The impact of RMB appreciation

2.2 Ask the students to discuss their answers to these questions in pairs, giving reasons. Answers will depend on students, especially in relation to question b.

Abstract E is quite good because it focuses on exactly what the presentation will talk about. It doesn't include any background information on the topic, but sufficient information is given in the description of the talk. Abstract D also does this, but because there is a lot of terminology used, it may be inaccessible to some readers.

2.3 Explain that the number of words a conference speaker can use for an abstract is restricted. This is usually because the conference programme has only very limited space for each speaker to outline the key points of their paper.

Set a limit of 60 words. Encourage students to begin with key words from their project. They should then draft and redraft their abstract as necessary, so that they say all they have to say concisely and effectively within the word limit.

2.4 Answers depend on students.

Task 3	**Preparing an oral presentation**

The amount of guidance that students receive on giving presentations can vary widely from department to department of a university. There is also variation in the methods and criteria for assessing presentations. Students on a pre-sessional course are given opportunities to develop presentation skills in a dedicated 'Spoken Language' class. For this reason, the work on oral presentation skills in this book is limited. Students are simply reminded about the use of note cards, OHTs and posters in the rest of this unit.

It might be most appropriate for students to give an oral presentation about an aspect of their project, rather than trying to describe the whole project. One way of doing this is to organize a mini-conference towards the end of the course, where each student gives a presentation in front of his/her peers and teachers. For example, 10–12 minutes could be allowed for each presentation, with three minutes for questions. Depending on numbers and time, this can be organized in parallel sessions over a single day, or sequentially over several days.

An alternative would be for individuals to present stages of their project to smaller groups. This can be an effective way for students to keep to deadlines and for them to focus on the content and organization of their project as they progress through the various stage of drafting.

There might be sufficient time for both the end-of-course conference and the ongoing approach to be implemented. See Appendix 8a on page 97 for a Presentation assessment form.

3.1 Give students time to think about the text in the information panels. Ask them to share their answers in small groups to the questions given.

3.2 Ask the students to study and discuss the note card and their answers to the questions in pairs or small groups. Point out that:
- note form is used
- there is plenty of space between each note for ease of reference

Explain that note cards can be very effective resources. They can be used when giving presentations, but also for noting bibliographical details in the library, examination revision notes, etc.

The students might want to consider using different forms of notation to help them differentiate between types of information as they work through their presentation, i.e., a main heading followed by *a*, *b*, *c* = main points. They might also want to consider using different colours to show different types of information or to highlight important words or phrases.

3.3 For this task, you might want to give students the opportunity to work on their own presentations, rather than focusing on one of the topics here. Alternatively, you could ask the students to work in groups and develop one of the note cards for one of the topics together.

Go through their note cards as a class. Some of the things you might want to feed back on include:
- amount of information on the cards – is there enough/too much?
- size and spacing of the text – is it easy to read?
- have they used different colours/places on the cards for different types of information?

Task 4	Editing your presentation slides

4.1 The students could do this individually and then compare their answers in pairs or small groups. The students can use the information panel in Ex 4.2 to help them decide what needs to be changed.

Ask students to look at the slides and suggest improvements. Explain that there are mistakes in each of the slides including spelling mistakes, the wrong use of words and distracting layout.

Answers:

Slide 1
- spelling mistakes: sustainability and worlds
- wrong use of 'roll', i.e., 'roles'

Slide 2
- *sustainability* is misspelt on parts of the slide, but correctly spelt on one occasion
- the content is overcrowded with far too much text. The likely results would be that the audience would either tend to read or try to read the slide rather than listen to the presenter, or the presenter might be tempted to read out the contents and thus fail to make eye contact with the audience and/or fail to engage with the audience.
- each point begins with a subject word which is inappropriate as the heading begins 'sustainability is …'

<u>Slide 3</u>
- spelling mistakes: sustainability and conclusion
- no bullet points
- varied and incorrect punctuation (no punctuation is necessary with bulleted points on a slide)
- a mixture of upper- and lower-case words which can be distracting
- unnecessary variation in font colour which can be distracting and difficult to read

<u>Slide 4</u>
- grammar mistake in title
- the photograph used is unnecessary as it doesn't provide any additional information or clearly illustrate the point being made. Students should not waste time finding photographs/images/diagrams unless they contribute to the presentation or are relevant to the information being given on that slide.

Finally, ask students to recreate more appropriate versions of the same slides.

4.2   If they haven't already, ask the students to read through the notes given in the information panel. They can then use this information and the answers you have discussed in Ex 4.1 to rewrite the slides. If time is limited, you could assign one or two slides per group and then ask them to share their rewritten slides with the rest of the class.

Task 5	**Preparing a poster presentation**

INPUT Preparing a poster presentation

Before introducing this Input panel, you might like to ask students if they have seen or given poster presentations before and what their thoughts are about them. This is a good point at which to discuss the difference between oral and poster presentations. With a poster presentation, the poster must do most of the 'talking'. Therefore, how the material is presented, and the clarity and attractiveness of presentation, are crucial. Explain to students that if they are required to give a poster presentation, it is their role to act as the presenter: to answer questions and provide further detail and support their project work, their findings and arguments.

Highlight the usefulness of figures, tables, graphs and images in poster presentations to break up the text and make it more visually interesting. They can also save space and remove the need for explanatory text.

5.1   Ask the students to work in pairs to begin planning their poster presentation. It would be a good idea for them to plan the layout on a piece of A4 paper before they begin working on their actual poster.

Go through the suggested format with them and highlight again the different sections that they might want to include.

Task 6	**Editing your written work**

Students often submit a final draft of their project without checking it carefully. This is usually down to poor time-management skills and the pressure to complete work before the end of the course. Emphasize the fact that even native speakers must allow time for editing and checking their work carefully.

6.1   Ask the students to work first individually and then in pairs to compile a list of things that they need to check at the editing stage of their project.

6.2   Students check their answers against the checklist given in the table.

You may want to highlight the format of the title page shown here and/or discuss the general conventions that are followed by the institutions where the students are studying. It is worth pointing out that this kind of formatting can be specific to the institution or even individual departments.

Note that a project evaluation form is included as a photocopiable handout in Appendix 8b on pages 98–99. You can use this two-page form to give feedback to students.

Unit summary

1   **Answers:**
a. general
b. background
c. aims
d. subject
e. real
f. text
g. research
h. results
i. thesis
j. definition

2   **Answers:**
Answers depend on students.

3   **Possible answer:**
Using note cards is a good idea because <u>they help you to organize your presentation / help you to remember the key points that you want to make.</u>

4   **Answers:**
A poster presentation must be clear and <u>concise</u>. The main point must be immediately clear to your <u>audience</u>, so you need to think carefully about <u>impact</u>. You must be selective – if you try to communicate too many ideas, your <u>point</u> will be lost.

5   **Possible answers:**
a. Use headings to guide your reader. / Number headings correctly.
b. Make sure you acknowledge all references.
c. Arrange your bibliography appropriately. / Make sure it is in alphabetical order.
d. Exchange your project with a classmate for language checking.
e. Check that each section is linked to the previous and following section.
f. Check that your introduction and conclusion are linked to your title.
g. Make sure you have responded to previous feedback.

6   **Answers:**
Answers depend on students, but it would be a good idea to go over their answers to this question in one-to-one tutorials.

Appendix 8a

Presentation assessment form

| Name: | Overall grade: |
| Title: | Tutor: |

	Profile A	Profile B	Profile C	Profile D
Delivery	Pronunciation hardly interferes with comprehension. Volume and speed are appropriate. Rhythm and intonation are varied and appropriate. Good eye contact.	Pronunciation of individual words occasionally interferes with comprehension. Volume and speed are adequate. Rhythm and intonation generally appropriate. Eye contact may be limited.	Pronunciation of chunks of language at times makes comprehension impossible. Volume/speed may be inadequate, and there is little or no eye contact. May be inappropriate use of gesture.	Pronunciation and intonation frequently impede comprehension, making it difficult to evaluate the presentation. May be inaudible.
Language	Clear evidence of ability to express complex ideas, using a wide range of appropriate vocabulary. Cohesive devices, where used, contribute to fluency. High degree of grammatical accuracy.	Some ability to express complex ideas, although not consistently. Reasonable use of range of vocabulary and structures. Cohesive devices, where used, contribute to fluency, but are sometimes misapplied.	Range of vocabulary and structures are adequate to express simple ideas. Errors sometimes impede communication.	Very limited range of vocabulary and grammar means ideas are expressed with difficulty. Presentation is often repetitive, due to insufficient control of language.
Organization	Strong introduction, with clear outline. Logical ordering of main points. Effective conclusion.	Generally, there is a logical ordering of main ideas. Introduction/conclusion are linked with main points.	Presentation lacks clear organization of ideas, making it difficult to follow.	Lack of any apparent organization makes it difficult to follow presentation.
Content	Content is appropriate and relevant. Topic is explored in sufficient depth.	Content is mostly appropriate and relevant.	Content is at times irrelevant, and development of ideas is superficial.	Content is not always related to the topic and there is little development of ideas.
Evidence of preparation	Evidence of thorough familiarity with topic. Fluent delivery, with skilful use of notes. Deals well with questions. Use of PowerPoint/OHTs enhances the presentation.	Familiar with topic. Use of notes sometimes interferes with delivery of presentation. Use of PowerPoint at times distracts from presentation content, due to unclear script/ inappropriate pictures/poor timing.	Reasonable preparation. Organization mostly clear and logical. Acceptable use of visual aids. Some difficulty in dealing with questions.	Inadequate preparation, with little evidence of familiarity with subject. Visual aids unhelpful, unclear or ineffective. Too much focus on PowerPoint rather than basic content. Inability to deal with questions.

Comments:

PHOTOCOPIABLE

Written project evaluation form

Name:	Overall grade:
Title:	

Abilities in the following areas	Postgraduate level	Highly competent (A)	Reasonably competent (B)	Developing competence (C)	Lacks competence (D)
Writing a project in own subject area	Can choose an appropriate topic with a clear focus.				
Independent research skills	Can find a range of appropriate resources independently.				
Identifying relevant information	Can identify key relevant points from complex texts and use as evidence to support own ideas.				
Planning	Can make a detailed, clearly structured plan which shows grasp of key ideas.				
Establishing a focus for own essay	Can establish a clear focus with thesis statement.				
Essay structure – introduction/ thesis statement/ conclusion	Can write an effective introduction with a strong thesis statement. Can write a conclusion, summarizing/ commenting effectively.				
Organizing ideas	Can link ideas within text at paragraph level and between parts of project.				
Summarizing information	Can summarize or paraphrase ideas from complex texts accurately and succinctly, showing clear understanding, avoiding plagiarism.				
Synthesizing information	Can take ideas from several sources and combine them into a cohesive argument.				

PHOTOCOPIABLE

Abilities in the following areas	Postgraduate level	Highly competent (A)	Reasonably competent (B)	Developing competence (C)	Lacks competence (D)
Referring to sources	Can refer to sources appropriately using some reporting verbs.				
Voice	Can comment on sources and indicate viewpoint.				
In-text referencing	Can reference appropriately using APA author/date system.				
Writing end of text references or bibliography	Can compile a list of references correctly, following APA format for articles, books and Internet sources.				
Use of language	Can expresses complex ideas clearly, drawing on a wide range of language structures and vocabulary, used accurately.				
Content	Can discuss topic in depth, recognizing the complexities.				
Critical thinking – being evaluative	Can demonstrate this through maintaining a thesis throughout the essay, making connections between ideas, evaluating and discussing topic in depth.				
Response to feedback	Can understand feedback well, and incorporate suggestions into final draft.				
Presentation	Can present work appropriately (headings, font, page numbering, etc.)				
Dealing with tables and graphs	Can incorporate fully and use range of language to describe. Can comment on analytically and critically.				
Overall comments:					

PHOTOCOPIABLE